P9-DCB-983

This

Sandra Lee
semi-homemade.

20-minute meals

book belongs to:

....

Meredith® Books Des Moines, Iowa

Copyright © 2006 Sandra Lee Semi-Homemade® All rights reserved. Printed in the U.S.A.
Library of Congress Control Number 2006921317 ISBN-13: 978-0-696-23263-3 ISBN-10: 0-696-23263-4
Published by Meredith® Books. Des Moines, Iowa.

sem·i·home·made

adj. **1:** a stress-free solution-based formula that provides savvy shortcuts and affordable, timesaving tips for overextended do-it-yourself homemakers **2:** a quick and easy equation wherein 70% ready-made convenience products are added to 30% fresh ingredients with creative personal style, allowing homemakers to take 100% of the credit for something that looks, feels, or tastes homemade **3:** a foolproof resource for having it all—and having the time to enjoy it **4:** a method created by Sandra Lee for home, garden, crafts, beauty, food, fashion, and entertaining wherein everything looks, tastes, and feels as if it was made from scratch.

Solution-based **E**nterprise that **M**otivates, **I**nspires, and **H**elps **O**rganize and **M**anage time, while **E**nriching **M**odern life by **A**dding **D**ependable shortcuts **E**veryday.

dedication

To Colleen and Kimber
the two most amazing women I know.
You keep me quick on my feet and full in my heart!

special thanks

To my fabulous friends, supportive and sweet one and all
Alexandra, Bonnie, Cari, Carol, Cassandra, Cindy, Farideh, Ghada,
Jane, Judy, Judith, Karen, Linda, Lisa, Mary, Patti, Peggy, and Vinnie

acknowledgments

Kudos and undying gratitude to the Quick Crew,
who routinely do the impossible in 20 minutes or less!
Jeff: Culinary Director, Pamela, Mark, Laurent, Michael, Linda, and Valerie

and

To the swiftest team in publishing, my production pals at Meredith
Jack, Bob, Doug, Jim, Jeff, Ken, Jan, Mick, and Jessica

You all deserve a big toast of cheer.

Here's to "Cocktail Time!"

Table of Contents

Chapter 1

Pasta
16

Chapter 2

Meat
66

Letter from Sandra

We all want our lives to be full and exciting, but sometimes they can seem too full. Life can feel like an endless cycle of obligations and pressures, places to be, and stuff to do. The things we have to do so often slip ahead of the things we want to do.

I love cooking, but it's become harder and harder to fit cooking into my schedule, or even eating, come to think of it. Everybody I know seems to be just as chronically time challenged as I, so I set out to lighten our load with a collection of quick half-hour recipes. Then I had lunch with my friend Susan. "I wish I had 30 minutes to cook!" Susan said. "I feel lucky if I have 20." And I thought, "You know what, she's right!" And so 20-minute meals was born. When life gets hectic, even ten minutes can make a difference!

Instead of taking 20 minutes for takeout or defrosting another frozen dinner, the same amount of time lets you prepare and serve a delicious and healthful Semi-Homemade® meal. Semi-Homemade® makes quick work of meal prep with my unique 70/30 philosophy: Buy 70% ready-made foods from the supermarket, add 30% of your own fresh ingredients and creative touches, and take 100% of the credit for a meal that looks, smells, and tastes gourmet.

I believe in living life to the fullest, and to do that, you have to take shortcuts, trading in the pursuit of perfection to meet the demands of reality. Nobody's perfect—and we don't need to be. Semi-Homemade® lets you be the best you can be, with whatever time you have. Let go of your preconceptions: Those feelings that you're somehow cheating yourself—or your family—by using packaged ingredients, forget them. Remember, instead of giving in, you're actually trading up, bypassing the drive-through for a healthful home-cooked meal.

From small starters to a sweet finish, this repertoire of recipes serves up months of complete, well-rounded meals that take you from in the door to on the table in just 20 minutes. Main dishes and sides are conveniently paired, so you don't waste precious time trying to figure out what goes with what. There are recipes to please both experienced cooks and beginners, meat lovers and vegetarians. There are spicy dishes, sweet dishes, heavy dishes, and light dishes; recipes for pastas, seafood, poultry, and beef; even desserts to give every meal a happy ending. You'll also find helpful hints and timesaving tricks to help you cut corners without cutting quality or taste.

Semi-Homemade® is all about getting that "made from scratch" taste with a realistic amount of energy and effort. Life is short, and when you think about how much every minute with family and friends counts, you'll savor every shortcut.

Real meals for real life. That's what Semi-Homemade® is all about.

Cheers to happy, healthy meals—in 20 minutes or less!

Sandra Lee

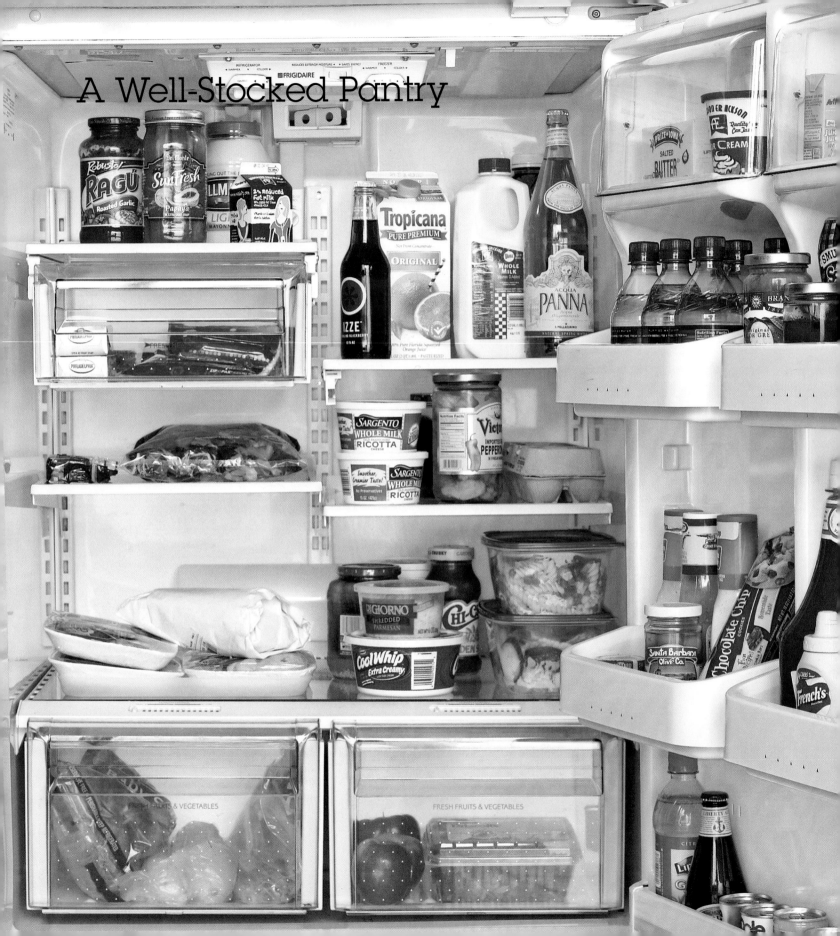

A Well-Stocked Pantry

Organize your refrigerator

It may seem easier to throw the groceries in the refrigerator and let them stay where they land, but you can save time in the long run by organizing a bit. Group similar items together, for instance put drinks on one shelf and snacks and small containers on another shelf. If you consistently put certain foods in the same place, it will save time when you're searching for an ingredient or item.

Place less perishable and less frequently used items, such as butter and eggs, near the back of the refrigerator. These foods may not stay as fresh if stored on the door due to drastic temperature changes when the door is opened. Keep perishable foods, such as leftovers, stacked in the front. Condiments can go on door shelves and fruits and vegetables should go in the produce drawers.

A Pantry Hutch

In my opinion, you can never have too much of your favorite foods on hand! I like to stock up on frequently used canned, boxed, and bottled products to make shopping lists shorter and meal preparation easier. When I need extra room for my packaged foods and cookbooks, I display them on the top shelves of an attractive wooden hutch. I then use the bottom shelves of the hutch to store small appliances, such as toasters and slow cookers.

An Organized Kitchen

Save time by becoming a kitchen-organizing guru! Little steps—such as keeping all your frequently used utensils in a container on the countertop—will make cooking a breeze.

Tray for bottles

Extra measuring cups

Notebooks

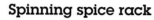

Everything has a place

Kitchen organization is the key to quick cooking. Keep bottles of seasonings on a tray in the cupboard—just pull the tray out to find what you're looking for quickly. Organize your kitchen gadget drawer by using dividers or trays with dividers. Purchase extra sets of the utensils you use most often, such as measuring spoons and cups. Have a notebook on hand to jot down grocery lists and other notes. Purchase a spinning spice rack and organize it so spices are easy to locate.

Spinning spice rack

Organized gadget drawer

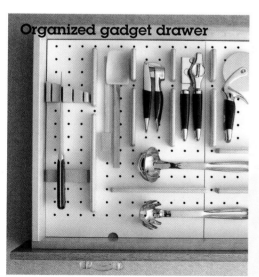

Timesaving Kitchen Gadgets

Pack your cupboards with must-have cooking gadgets and appliances! These products—such as a good pair of kitchen shears for snipping herbs—save loads of time and energy.

Salad spinner

Food processor

Egg slicer

Immersion blender

Microwave oven

Ice cream scooper

Smart cooks have:

Ice cream scoopers are for so much more than ice cream! Use them to create uniform-size and cookies and meatballs.

Immersion blenders puree soups right in the pot! This is more efficient than a regular blender that can only blend small batches at one time and can be dangerous when filled with hot liquid.

Salad spinners make washing and drying salad greens quick and easy.

Food processors can do so much! Use them to make cracker and bread crumbs and chop peppers and onions. Do double duty with the food processor by chopping extra of these foods, then seal in freezer bags and freeze for later.

Egg slicers can be used to slice other soft foods, such as strawberries, mushrooms, and peeled kiwifruit.

Microwave ovens are invaluable when time is of the essence. Not only do they melt butter and chocolate quickly and efficiently, they can also toast nuts in minutes! Spread an even layer of chopped nuts in a glass pie plate, then microwave on high for 2 minutes, stirring nuts every 30 seconds.

13

Quick Cleanup

Kick kitchen cleanup into high gear by thinking ahead! A quick trick: spray measuring cups with nonstick cooking spray before filling with sticky ingredients such as honey.

Foil-lined pan for bars

Disposable foil pans

Foil-lined baking pans

Make life easier

Tidying up the kitchen is simple with a little planning. When making bar cookies or other messy foods, line the pan with foil for easy removal and even easier cleanup. Or use disposable foil pans and just throw the mess away when you're done cooking! Grate cheese and citrus zest, peel vegetables, and sprinkle sugar on cookies over waxed paper. This keeps the mess in one place and makes it easier to clean the counter when you're done. Use a zip-top plastic bag to marinate meats and combine messy mixtures. Toss the bag and cleanup is done!

Waxed paper

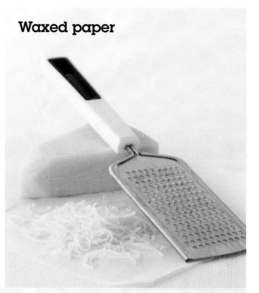

Resealable zip-top bag

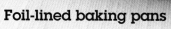

Pasta

In Italy, pasta symbolizes love. In Asia, it symbolizes artistry. I combine the two into a delicious presentation that's easy enough for every day yet beautiful enough for company. The trick is to keep the pasta shape and sauce harmonious. Linguine and other thin pastas and noodles work well with delicate sauces, such as creamy Newburg or light miso. Thicker pastas—fettuccine, ravioli, and penne—are best balanced with chunkier sauces, such as spicy chicken Alfredo or hearty Sicilian pesto. This chapter features noodles of all shapes and sizes teamed with sauces that surprise and delight the taste buds. Delicate cream sauce is spiked with ancho peppers, clams are paired with smoky pancetta, tangy sausage is sweetened with shrimp. Sumptuous side dishes, such as Three-Tomato Salad, Prosciutto-Parmesan Biscuits, and Five-Spice Eggplant, round out each meal perfectly.

The Meals

Penne à la Vodka

Start to Finish 15 minutes
Makes 6 servings

Serving Ideas:
Roasted Asparagus
with Olives (page 20)

Store-bought crusty
French bread

The interplay of tomato and cream renders an elegant light red sauce with the subtle tang of vodka. A side of Roasted Asparagus with Olives complements with both color and crunch.

1	box (16-ounce) dried penne pasta, *Barilla®*
1	tablespoon extra-virgin olive oil, *Bertolli®*
3	ounces pancetta, diced
$\frac{1}{2}$	cup vodka, *Absolut®*
1	jar (26-ounce) pasta sauce, *Prego® Traditional*
$\frac{1}{2}$	cup grated Parmesan cheese, *DiGiorno®* (plus more for garnish, optional)
$\frac{1}{3}$	cup whipping cream

1. In a large pot of boiling salted water, cook pasta according to package directions. Drain well; return to hot pot. Cover; keep warm.

2. Meanwhile, in a large saucepan, heat olive oil over medium-high heat. Add pancetta to hot oil; cook and stir until pancetta is browned. Add vodka to saucepan, scraping up any browned bits in the bottom of pan. Add pasta sauce. Bring to a boil; reduce heat to low. Stir in the $\frac{1}{2}$ cup grated Parmesan cheese. Simmer sauce about 5 minutes. Stir whipping cream into saucepan.

3. Serve sauce hot over cooked pasta. Garnish with additional grated Parmesan cheese (optional).

Roasted Asparagus with Olives

Start to Finish 20 minutes
Makes 6 servings

1 ½ pounds asparagus, trimmed
½ cup kalamata olives, pitted, *Peloponnese®*
1 tablespoon extra-virgin olive oil, *Bertolli®*
1 teaspoon lemon pepper, *Lawry's®*

1. Preheat oven to 425 degrees F. Line a baking sheet with aluminum foil.

2. Place asparagus and olives on prepared baking sheet. Drizzle with olive oil; sprinkle with lemon pepper. Toss to coat asparagus and olives.

3. Roast in preheated oven for 10 to 12 minutes or until asparagus is crisp-tender.

Mini Penne with
Spicy Chicken Alfredo

Start to Finish 20 minutes
Makes 4 servings

Serving Ideas:

Mediterranean Mixed
Vegetables (page 24)

Prewashed spring lettuce
mix with bottled balsamic
vinaigrette

8	ounces dried mini penne pasta, *Barilla*®
1	jar (16-ounce) Alfredo sauce, *Classico*®
1	can (14.5-ounce) diced tomatoes with basil, garlic, and oregano, *Del Monte*®
1	tablespoon Italian seasoning, *McCormick*®
$\frac{1}{2}$	teaspoon red pepper flakes, *McCormick*®
2	packages (6 ounces each) refrigerated cooked chicken breast strips, *Oscar Mayer*® or *Louis Rich*®
1	can (2.25-ounce) sliced black olives, drained, *Early California*® Shredded Parmesan cheese, *Kraft*®

1. In a large pot of boiling salted water, cook pasta according to package directions. Drain well; return to hot pot. Cover; keep warm.

2. Meanwhile, in a medium saucepan, combine Alfredo sauce, tomatoes, Italian seasoning, and red pepper flakes over medium heat. Stir in chicken and olives. Bring to a simmer; cook for 10 minutes.

3. Serve hot over cooked pasta. Top with Parmesan cheese.

Mediterranean
Mixed Vegetables

Start to Finish 10 minutes
Makes 4 servings

Take a virtual trip to the sunny Mediterranean tonight! Vegetables get a kick that's second to none with tangy capers and a can of diced tomatoes with herbs. This is a delicious way to add healthful, vitamin-packed broccoli, cauliflower, and carrots to your diet.

1   package (16-ounce) loose-pack frozen mixed vegetables (broccoli, cauliflower, carrots)
1   can (14.5-ounce) diced tomatoes with basil, garlic, and oregano, *Del Monte*®
1   tablespoon capers, drained

1. In a microwave-safe bowl, combine frozen mixed vegetables, tomatoes, and drained capers. Cover with plastic wrap; microwave on high setting (100% power) for 6 to 8 minutes, stirring halfway through cooking time.

*NOTE: Another time, give this dish a whole new flavor by using a different package of mixed vegetables. Great mixtures include baby peas, baby carrots, snow peas, and baby corn or Brussels sprouts, cauliflower, and carrots. If you can't find a mixture with all your favorite vegetables, try mixing and matching to create a colorful combination of your own.

Gnocchi and Chicken with Roasted Garlic and Gorgonzola Cream

Start to Finish 20 minutes
Makes 4 servings

Serving Ideas:
Zucchini Oreganata
(page 28)

Packaged Caesar
salad

Gnocchi, small potato dumplings, offer a tasty change of pace from pasta and risotto. Minced garlic and Gorgonzola cheese guarantee a pleasantly pungent bite to the cream sauce. Finish the plate with verdant Zucchini Oreganata.

1	box (16-ounce) potato gnocchi, *Alessi*®
1	whole roasted chicken (about 2 pounds)*
2 ¼	cups milk (plus extra to thin sauce, if necessary)
1	packet (1.8-ounce) white sauce mix, *Knorr*®
6	ounces crumbled Gorgonzola cheese, *Treasure Cave*® (plus more for garnish, optional)
1	tablespoon bottled minced roasted garlic, *Christopher Ranch*® Fresh parsley leaves (optional)

1. In a large pot of boiling salted water, cook gnocchi for 3 to 4 minutes or until gnocchi float to the surface. Drain well. Return gnocchi to hot pot. Cover; keep warm. Meanwhile, remove meat from roasted chicken; shred into bite-size pieces.

2. In a medium saucepan, whisk together milk and white sauce mix over medium-high heat. Bring to a boil, stirring constantly. Reduce heat to low. Add Gorgonzola cheese and garlic. Simmer for 2 to 3 minutes more or until sauce thickens, stirring occasionally. Remove from heat. (If sauce is too thick, add a small amount of milk to reach desired consistency.)

3. Add shredded chicken to gnocchi. Pour sauce over gnocchi and chicken. Toss to combine. Garnish with parsley and additional crumbled Gorgonzola cheese (optional). Serve hot.

*NOTE: Purchase a whole roasted chicken at the deli counter of your supermarket.

Zucchini Oreganata

Start to Finish 15 minutes
Makes 4 servings

2	tablespoons extra-virgin olive oil, *Bertolli®*
1½	pounds zucchini, cut into ¼-inch slices
1	can (14.5-ounce) diced tomatoes with basil, garlic, and oregano, *Del Monte®*
1	tablespoon finely chopped fresh oregano or 1 teaspoon dried oregano, *McCormick®*
	Salt
	Ground black pepper
	Fresh oregano sprigs (optional)

1. In a large skillet, heat olive oil over medium-high heat. Add zucchini to hot oil; cook and stir for 3 to 4 minutes. Add tomatoes and oregano. Bring to a boil; reduce heat. Simmer for 5 to 7 minutes or until zucchini slices are crisp-tender.

2. Season with salt and pepper to taste. Garnish with fresh oregano sprigs (optional). Serve hot.

Chicken Ravioli with Ancho Cream Sauce

Start to Finish 20 minutes
Makes 4 servings

Serving Ideas:
Three-Tomato Salad
with Creamy Avocado
Dressing (page 32)

Store-bought garlic bread

2	packages (9 ounces each) refrigerated chicken and roasted garlic ravioli, *Buitoni®*
1	jar (16-ounce) Alfredo sauce, *Classico®*
1	can (14.5-ounce) fire-roasted diced tomatoes, *Muir Glen®*
1½	teaspoons ancho chile powder, *McCormick®*
½	teaspoon poultry seasoning, *McCormick®*
	Shredded Parmesan cheese, *Kraft®*

1. In a large pot of boiling salted water, cook ravioli according to package directions. Drain well; return to hot pot. Cover; keep warm.

2. Meanwhile, in a medium saucepan, combine Alfredo sauce, tomatoes, chile powder, and poultry seasoning. Bring to a simmer over medium heat; reduce heat to low.

3. Toss warm ravioli with sauce. Remove from heat. Serve hot with Parmesan cheese.

Three-Tomato Salad with Creamy Avocado Dressing

Start to Finish 15 minutes
Makes 4 servings

8	ounces vine-ripened red tomatoes,* cut into bite-size pieces
8	ounces vine-ripened yellow tomatoes,* cut into bite-size pieces
8	ounces vine-ripened orange tomatoes,* cut into bite-size pieces
	Salt
	Ground black pepper
1	cup purchased guacamole dip, *Dean's*®
1	cup whipping cream
1	tablespoon bottled lemon juice, *ReaLemon*®
	Pinch cayenne, *McCormick*®

1. In a medium bowl, combine tomatoes. Season with salt and pepper; set aside.

2. For dressing, in a small bowl, stir together guacamole dip, whipping cream, lemon juice, and cayenne.

3. Serve tomatoes with dressing.

*NOTE: When heirloom tomatoes are in season, use different varieties purchased from the farmer's market.

Fettuccine with Mushroom Sauce

Start to Finish 20 minutes
Makes 4 servings

Serving Ideas:

Caesar Salad with Creamy Roasted Garlic Dressing and Parmesan Crisps (page 36)

Store-bought focaccia bread

2	packages (9 ounces each) refrigerated fettuccine, *Buitoni*®
3	tablespoons extra-virgin olive oil, *Bertolli*®
1	package (8-ounce) presliced fresh white button mushrooms
1	package (8-ounce) presliced fresh brown mushrooms
1	cup frozen chopped onions, *Ore-Ida*®
1½	cups reduced-sodium beef broth, *Swanson*®
⅓	cup dry sherry, *Christian Brothers*®
¼	cup balsamic vinegar
1	packet (1.5-ounce) beef stew seasoning, *McCormick*®
1	can (14.5-ounce) diced tomatoes with garlic and onion, drained, *Del Monte*®
	Flat-leaf parsley, chopped (optional)

1. In a large pot of boiling salted water, cook pasta according to package directions. Drain well; return to hot pot. Cover; keep warm.

2. Meanwhile, in a large skillet, heat olive oil over medium-high heat. Add mushrooms and frozen onions to hot oil; cook and stir for 7 to 8 minutes.

3. Create a well in center of the mushroom mixture. Add beef broth, sherry, and balsamic vinegar. Stir in beef stew seasoning until dissolved. Add drained tomatoes. Bring to a boil; reduce heat. Simmer for 5 to 6 minutes.

4. Garnish with parsley (optional). Serve hot over cooked pasta.

Caesar Salad with Creamy Roasted Garlic Dressing and Parmesan Crisps

Start to Finish 20 minutes
Makes 4 servings

FOR PARMESAN CRISPS:

- ½ cup shredded Parmesan cheese, *Kraft®*

FOR CREAMY ROASTED GARLIC DRESSING:

- ½ cup Caesar salad dressing, *Wish-Bone®*
- ¼ cup mayonnaise, *Hellmann's®* or *Best Foods®*
- 4 cloves bottled roasted garlic, *Christopher Ranch®*

FOR CAESAR SALAD:

- 1 bag (10-ounce) romaine hearts, chopped, *Fresh Express®*
- 1 cup seasoned croutons, *Marie Callender's®*

1. Preheat broiler. Line a baking sheet with aluminum foil.

2. For Parmesan Crisps, place a 3-inch ring mold* on prepared baking sheet. Sprinkle 1 tablespoon of the Parmesan cheese into the mold. Carefully remove mold. Repeat three more times so there are four Parmesan circles. Broil 6 inches from heat for 3 to 4 minutes, watching carefully until crisps turn golden brown. Remove from broiler; cool on wire rack. Carefully peel crisps from foil.

3. For Creamy Roasted Garlic Dressing, in a blender, combine Caesar salad dressing, mayonnaise, and roasted garlic. Cover and blend on medium speed until combined.

4. For Caesar Salad, in a large bowl, combine romaine hearts, croutons, and the remaining ¼ cup Parmesan cheese. Toss with dressing.

5. Serve salad on 4 plates. Garnish with Parmesan Crisps.

*NOTE: If you don't have a ring mold, you can substitute an 8-ounce pineapple can with the top and bottom removed.

Fettuccine with Sausage and Shrimp

Start to Finish 20 minutes
Makes 4 servings

Serving Ideas:
Parmesan Garlic
Toast (below)

Chopped romaine
hearts with bottled
creamy Caesar dressing

2	packages (9 ounces each) refrigerated fettuccine, *Buitoni*®
2	tablespoons extra-virgin olive oil, *Bertolli*®
8	ounces spicy Italian sausage, casings removed
1	package (8-ounce) presliced fresh white button mushrooms
2	teaspoons bottled crushed garlic, *Christopher Ranch*®
2	tablespoons butter
1¼	cups milk
1	package (1.3-ounce) tomato sauce mix, *Knorr*®
12	ounces cooked peeled and deveined medium shrimp
1	can (2.25-ounce) sliced black olives, drained, *Early California*®

1. In a large pot of boiling water, cook pasta according to package directions. Drain well; return to hot pot. Cover; keep warm. Meanwhile, in a large skillet, heat olive oil over medium-high heat. Add sausage, mushrooms, and garlic to hot oil; cook for 7 to 8 minutes or until sausage is browned, stirring occasionally.

2. Create a well in the center of the sausage mixture; add butter. When butter has melted, add milk. Stir in tomato sauce mix until dissolved. Bring to a boil. Reduce heat to low. Stir in shrimp and drained olives; simmer for 4 to 5 minutes or until sauce thickens and shrimp are heated through. Serve hot over cooked pasta.

Parmesan Garlic Toast

Start to Finish 20 minutes
Makes 4 servings

6	French rolls, split in half, *Sara Lee*® (or 6 hoagie buns)
½	stick (¼ cup) butter, melted
1	teaspoon bottled crushed garlic, *Christopher Ranch*®
½	teaspoon Italian seasoning, *McCormick*®
½	cup grated Parmesan cheese, *DiGiorno*®

1. Preheat oven to 450 degrees F. Place French rolls, cut sides up, on a baking sheet; set aside.

2. In a small bowl, combine melted butter, garlic, and Italian seasoning. Brush French rolls with butter mixture. Sprinkle with Parmesan cheese. Bake in preheated oven for 10 to 12 minutes. Serve hot.

Linguine with Newburg Sauce

Start to Finish 15 minutes
Makes 4 servings

Serving Ideas:
Roasted Tomatoes Gratin
(page 43)

Store-bought crusty
sourdough bread

2	packages (9 ounces each) refrigerated linguine, *Buitoni®*
6	tablespoons butter
2	stalks celery, sliced
½	medium onion, diced
½	cup white wine
1	packet (2-ounce) Newburg sauce mix, *Knorr®*
¾	cup milk
12	ounces cooked peeled and deveined medium shrimp
1	can (6-ounce) lump crabmeat, *Crown Prince®*

1. In a large pot of boiling salted water, cook pasta according to package directions. Drain well; return to hot pot. Cover; keep warm.

2. Meanwhile, in a large saucepan, melt butter over medium-high heat. Add celery and onion; cook and stir for 5 to 6 minutes or until soft.

3. Stir in white wine. Stir in sauce mix until dissolved. Stir in milk. Bring to a boil; reduce heat. Simmer for 2 minutes. Add shrimp and crabmeat to the wine mixture; heat through.

4. Serve hot over cooked pasta.

Roasted Tomatoes Gratin

Start to Finish 20 minutes
Makes 4 servings

A gratin is delectably French—which is why these garlic-perfumed tomato halves make such an engaging accompaniment to cream-sauce dishes, such as Linguine with Newburg Sauce.

4	medium tomatoes, cut in half
	Salt
	Ground black pepper
$\frac{1}{4}$	cup garlic and herb bread crumbs, *Progresso*®
$\frac{1}{4}$	cup grated Parmesan cheese, *DiGiorno*®
2	tablespoons butter, melted
1	teaspoon bottled crushed garlic, *Christopher Ranch*®

1. Preheat oven to 450 degrees F. Line a baking sheet with aluminum foil.

2. Place tomato halves, cut sides up, on prepared baking sheet. Season with salt and pepper; set aside.

3. In a small bowl, combine bread crumbs, Parmesan cheese, butter, and garlic. Spoon over tomatoes.

4. Roast tomatoes in preheated oven for 10 to 12 minutes or until bread crumb mixture is golden brown.

Linguine with Clams and Pancetta

Start to Finish 20 minutes
Makes 4 servings

Serving Ideas:
Prosciutto-Parmesan
Biscuits (below)

Packaged Caesar
salad mix

2	packages (9 ounces each) refrigerated linguine, *Buitoni®*
3	ounces pancetta, diced
1	cup frozen chopped onion, *Ore-Ida®*
1	tablespoon butter
2	cans (6.5 ounces each) chopped clams, *Snow's®*
¾	cup white wine
1	packet (1.6-ounce) garlic herb sauce mix, *Knorr®*
1	tablespoon bottled lemon juice, *ReaLemon®*

1. In a large pot of boiling salted water, cook pasta according to package directions. Drain well; return to hot pot. Cover; keep warm.

2. Meanwhile, in a large skillet, cook pancetta for 4 to 5 minutes over medium heat, stirring frequently. Add frozen onion and butter; cook and stir about 5 minutes more or until onion is soft.

3. Drain clams, reserving clam juice. Set clams aside. Add reserved clam juice and white wine to skillet. Stir in garlic herb sauce mix until dissolved. Bring mixture to a boil; reduce heat to low. Add clams and lemon juice. Simmer for 3 to 4 minutes or until heated through. Serve hot over cooked pasta.

Prosciutto-Parmesan Biscuits

Start to Finish 20 minutes
Makes 12 biscuits

2¼	cups baking mix, *Bisquick®*
3	ounces prosciutto, finely chopped
⅔	cup whipping cream
½	teaspoon ground black pepper
	Extra-virgin olive oil, *Bertolli®*
	Grated Parmesan cheese, *DiGiorno®*

1. Preheat oven to 450 degrees F. In a large bowl, combine baking mix, prosciutto, cream, and pepper; stir until just combined. On a lightly floured surface, knead dough 10 times; form into ball. Roll dough until ½ inch thick. Using a 2¼-inch round biscuit cutter, cut dough into rounds, pressing straight down (do not twist cutter).

2. Place biscuits on an ungreased baking sheet. Lightly brush tops with olive oil and sprinkle with Parmesan cheese. Bake for 10 minutes or until golden brown.

Spinach Pasta Caprese

Start to Finish 15 minutes
Makes 4 servings

Serving Ideas:
Shrimp and Scallop Salad with Mandarin-Poppy Seed Dressing (page 48)

Steamed broccoli

12   ounces (about 1⅓ packages, 9 ounces each) refrigerated spinach fettucine, *Buitoni*®
3   tablespoons extra-virgin olive oil, *Bertolli*®
1   teaspoon bottled crushed garlic, *Christopher Ranch*®
1   can (14.5-ounce) diced tomatoes, *Hunt's*®
8   ounces fresh mozzarella, torn into small pieces
15   large fresh basil leaves, cut into thin strips (plus more for garnish, optional)
    Shredded Parmesan cheese, *Kraft*® (optional)

1. In a large pot of boiling salted water, cook pasta according to package directions. Drain well; return to hot pot. Toss with 2 tablespoons of the olive oil. Cover; keep warm.

2. In a large saucepan, heat the remaining 1 tablespoon olive oil over medium heat. Add garlic to hot oil; cook for 1 minute. Add tomatoes and bring to boil. Remove tomato mixture from heat and toss with pasta.

3. Add mozzarella and basil to pasta; toss to combine. Garnish with Parmesan cheese and additional fresh basil (optional).

Shrimp and Scallop Salad with Mandarin-Poppy Seed Dressing

Start to Finish 20 minutes
Makes 4 servings

4	ounces bay scallops
1	can (15-ounce) mandarin orange segments, *Dole®*
¼	cup poppy seed salad dressing, *Knott's®*
8	ounces cooked peeled and deveined bay or other small shrimp
4	cups prewashed baby arugula, *Ready Pac®*

1. In a small saucepan of simmering water, cook scallops for 3 to 4 minutes. Drain scallops. Immediately place scallops in a bowl of ice water for 1 to 2 minutes. Drain; set aside.

2. Drain orange segments, reserving 2 tablespoons juice. Set orange segments aside. In a medium bowl, combine reserved juice and poppy seed salad dressing. Add scallops, orange segments, and shrimp to dressing mixture; toss to combine.

3. Divide arugula among 4 salad plates. Top with scallop mixture.

Sausage and Portobellos with Sicilian Pesto

Start to Finish 20 minutes
Makes 4 servings

Serving Ideas:
Fast and Easy Minestrone
(page 52)

Store-bought garlic bread

2	packages (9 ounces each) refrigerated fettuccine or linguine, *Buitoni®*
2	tablespoons extra-virgin olive oil, *Bertolli®*
3	links spicy Italian sausage, casings removed
2	teaspoons bottled minced garlic, *Christopher Ranch®*
2	portobello mushroom caps, cut in half and sliced
1	can (10-ounce) diced Italian tomatoes, drained, *Ro-Tel®*
1	container (7-ounce) refrigerated pesto with basil, *Buitoni®*

1. In a large pot of boiling salted water, cook pasta according to package directions. Drain well; return to hot pot. Cover; keep warm.

2. Meanwhile, in a large skillet, heat olive oil over medium-high heat. Add sausage and garlic to hot oil; cook and stir for 5 minutes, breaking up the sausage. Add mushrooms to skillet; cook and stir for 5 minutes more. Add drained tomatoes and pesto sauce. Bring to a boil; reduce heat. Simmer for 5 minutes.

3. Serve hot over cooked pasta.

Fast and Easy
Minestrone

Start to Finish 15 minutes
Makes 4 servings

Frozen vegetables, canned herbed tomatoes, and a port wine stock hustle you through the tedious prep minestrone requires. Serve it warm in winter and cool in summer with a more boisterous entrée such as Sausage and Portobellos with Sicilian Pesto.

1	tablespoon extra-virgin olive oil, *Bertolli*®
½	medium onion, chopped
1	teaspoon bottled minced garlic, *Christopher Ranch*®
½	cup port wine, *Hardys*®
1	container (32-ounce) reduced-sodium chicken broth, *Swanson*®
1	can (14.5-ounce) diced tomatoes with basil, garlic, and oregano, *Del Monte*®
7	ounces loose-pack frozen mixed vegetables (sugar snap peas, carrots, broccoli, cauliflower), *C&W*®
½	cup canned red kidney beans, rinsed and drained, *Bush's*®
1	teaspoon Italian seasoning, *McCormick*®
	Shredded Parmesan cheese, *Kraft*® (optional)

1. In a large saucepan, heat olive oil over medium-high heat. Add onion to hot oil; cook and stir for 1 minute. Add garlic and cook for 30 seconds more. Add port wine and bring to a boil. Reduce heat; simmer for 1 minute.

2. Add chicken broth, tomatoes, frozen mixed vegetables, kidney beans, and Italian seasoning. Bring to a boil. Reduce heat to a rapid simmer; cook for 5 to 10 minutes.

3. Serve hot with Parmesan cheese (optional).

Teriyaki Chicken Noodles

Start to Finish 20 minutes
Makes 4 servings

Serving Ideas:
Sugar Snap Peas with
Red Pepper (below)

6	**ounces somen noodles**
2	**tablespoons canola oil, *Wesson*®**
1½	**pounds chicken tenders, cut into bite-size pieces**
1	**bag (6-ounce) prewashed baby spinach, *Fresh Express*®**
1	**cup loose-pack frozen carrot slices, thawed, *C&W*®**
½	**cup teriyaki sauce, *Kikkoman*®**
½	**cup reduced-sodium chicken broth, *Swanson*®**
1	**teaspoon bottled crushed garlic, *Christopher Ranch*®**
1	**teaspoon bottled minced ginger, *Christopher Ranch*®**

1. In a large pot of boiling salted water, cook noodles for 3 minutes. Drain; rinse with cold water. Drain well; set aside.

2. Meanwhile, in a large skillet, heat canola oil over medium-high heat. Add chicken to hot oil; cook and stir about 7 minutes or until cooked through.

3. Add spinach, thawed carrots, teriyaki sauce, chicken broth, garlic, and ginger to skillet. Stir to combine; simmer over medium heat for 5 minutes. Add cooked noodles and toss to combine.

Sugar Snap Peas with Red Pepper

Start to Finish 10 minutes
Makes 4 servings

1	**bag (14-ounce) loose-pack frozen sugar snap peas, *C&W*®**
¼	**cup roasted red bell pepper, cut into thin strips, *Delallo*®**
1	**teaspoon dark sesame oil**
2	**teaspoons sesame seeds**

1. In a microwave-safe bowl, combine frozen snap peas, red bell pepper, and sesame oil. Cover with plastic wrap; microwave on high setting (100% power) for 6 to 7 minutes, stirring halfway through cooking time.

2. Toss with sesame seeds. Serve hot.

Spicy Peanut Noodles

Start to Finish 15 minutes
Makes 4 servings

Serving Ideas:

Five-Spice Eggplant
(page 59)

Prewashed salad mix with
bottled Asian vinaigrette

8   ounces soba noodles
¾   cup peanut butter, *Laura Scudder's*®
½   cup reduced-sodium chicken broth, *Swanson*®
3   tablespoons honey, *Sue Bee*®
2   tablespoons dark sesame oil
2   tablespoons soy sauce, *Kikkoman*®
2   teaspoons Thai seasoning, *Spice Islands*®
¼   teaspoon red pepper flakes, *McCormick*®
¼   cup peanuts, chopped (optional)
1   scallion (green onion), sliced diagonally (optional)

1. In a large pot of boiling salted water, cook soba noodles for 4 to 5 minutes. Drain; rinse with cold water. Drain well; set aside.

2. For dressing, in a medium bowl, whisk together peanut butter, chicken broth, honey, sesame oil, soy sauce, Thai seasoning, and red pepper flakes. Pour dressing over soba noodles and toss to combine.

3. Garnish with chopped peanuts and sliced scallion (optional).

Five-Spice Eggplant

Start to Finish: 20 minutes
Makes: 4 servings

Vibrantly colored eggplant takes on delicious ethnic flavors when tossed with Asian five-spice powder—a snazzy side dish for **Spicy Peanut Noodles, page 56.** For an outstanding presentation, pile the noodles on a platter, then line the outside of the platter with overlapping eggplant slices. Beautiful!

4 small Japanese eggplants, cut into $\frac{1}{4}$-inch slices
1 tablespoon five-spice powder,* *McCormick®*
1 tablespoon canola oil, *Wesson®*
2 teaspoons dark sesame oil

1. Preheat oven to 400 degrees F. Line baking sheet with aluminum foil.

2. In a medium bowl, toss eggplant, five-spice powder, canola oil, and sesame oil. Lay eggplant slices on prepared baking sheet. Roast for 10 to 15 minutes or until tender.

*NOTE: Five-spice powder is a blend of five ground spices (cinnamon, cloves, fennel seeds, star anise, and Szechuan peppercorns) used in Asian cooking. You'll find it in the spice section of most large supermarkets.

Yakisoba Noodle Bowl with Shrimp

Start to Finish 20 minutes
Makes 4 servings

Serving Ideas:
Asian Slaw (page 62)

A soy-sesame broth sets a mellow backdrop for tenderly cooked shrimp and a float of vegetables. It might taste exotic, but the ingredients are straight from the grocery. Complete the meal with a tangy side of Asian Slaw.

1	container (32-ounce) reduced-sodium chicken broth, *Swanson*®
1	cup loose-pack frozen peas, *C&W*®
1	cup loose-pack frozen carrot slices, *C&W*®
1	tablespoon dark sesame oil
1	tablespoon soy sauce, *Kikkoman*®
1	tablespoon Szechuan stir-fry sauce, *San-J*®
17	ounces refrigerated yakisoba noodles, *Maruchan*®
1	pound cooked peeled and deveined medium shrimp

1. In a large pot, combine chicken broth, frozen peas, frozen carrots, sesame oil, soy sauce, and stir-fry sauce. Bring to a boil; reduce heat. Simmer for 6 minutes.

2. Add noodles and return to boiling. Reduce heat; simmer for 2 minutes. Add shrimp; simmer for 1 to 2 minutes or until shrimp are heated through.

3. Using tongs, divide noodles among 4 soup bowls. Add shrimp and ladle in broth.

Asian Slaw

Start to Finish 20 minutes
Makes 4 servings

$\frac{1}{4}$ cup rice vinegar, *Maruchan*®
1   tablespoon sesame seeds
1   tablespoon canola oil, *Wesson*®
1   tablespoon dark sesame oil
$\frac{1}{2}$ teaspoon sugar (optional)
12   ounces (about 5$\frac{1}{2}$ cups) three-color coleslaw mix, *Fresh Express*®
1   cup canned bean sprouts
1   cup chow mein noodles, *La Choy*® (plus more for garnish, optional)

1. In a large bowl, whisk together rice vinegar, sesame seeds, canola oil, sesame oil, and sugar (optional).

2. Add coleslaw mix, bean sprouts, and the 1 cup chow mein noodles. Toss to combine. Chill for 15 minutes to blend flavors.

3. Garnish with additional chow mein noodles (optional).

Miso Poached Tilapia with Udon Noodles

Start to Finish 20 minutes
Makes 4 servings

Serving Ideas:
Edamame Salad
with Wasabi Dressing
(below)

12 ounces udon noodles
3½ ounces fresh shiitake mushrooms (stems removed), sliced
3 scallions (green onions), sliced diagonally into ½-inch pieces
1 cup sake or white wine
2 tablespoons soy sauce, *Kikkoman*®
1 pound fresh tilapia fillets
1 container (32-ounce) organic miso broth, *Imagine*®

1. In a large pot of boiling salted water, cook thin noodles for 6 to 8 minutes or thicker noodles for 10 to 12 minutes. Drain well; return to hot pot. Cover; keep warm.

2. Meanwhile, in a large straight-sided skillet, combine mushrooms, scallions, sake, and soy sauce. Bring to boil over medium-high heat. Reduce heat to low. Add fish fillets. Cover; remove from heat. Let stand for 10 minutes.

3. In a medium saucepan, heat miso broth. Using tongs, divide noodles among 4 soups bowls; ladle broth into soup bowls. Top with tilapia.

Edamame Salad with Wasabi Dressing

Start to Finish 15 minutes
Makes 6 servings

1 bag (16-ounce) frozen shelled edamame (green soybeans), *C&W*®
2 tablespoons water
1 can (16-ounce) baby corn, drained and cut into
   ½-inch pieces, *Reece's*®
1 jar (2-ounce) sliced pimiento, drained, *Dromedary*®
4 radishes, thinly sliced
2 scallions (green onions), thinly sliced
FOR WASABI DRESSING:
⅓ cup Chinese chicken salad dressing, *Girard's*®
1 tablespoon soy sauce, *Kikkoman*®
1 teaspoon prepared wasabi,* *S&B*®

1. In a microwave-safe bowl, combine frozen edamame and the water. Cover with plastic wrap; cook on high setting (100% power) for 6 to 8 minutes, stirring halfway through cooking time. Let stand, covered, for 1 minute. Place edamame in ice water for 2 to 3 minutes. Drain well.

2. In a medium bowl, combine corn, pimiento, radishes, and scallions. Add edamame. For Wasabi Dressing, in a small bowl, combine salad dressing, soy sauce, and wasabi. Pour over salad and toss to combine.

*NOTE: If you are unable to find prepared wasabi in the Asian section of the grocery store, use wasabi powder mixed with a little water. Wasabi powder (*McCormick*®) is available in the spice section of the grocery store.

Meat

Like many Americans, I grew up on "meat and potatoes" dinners that included pot roast, hamburgers, and the occasional steak. Then I went to school in Wisconsin and discovered beer brats with kraut and smoked summer sausage. Eating out and trying different things opened my world to a plethora of meats and sauces, many of them too intimidating to attempt at home. This chapter makes it easy to branch out, with a diverse menu of bistro-type meals you can whip up quicker than it takes to pick up burgers. Spice up your weeknights with Chili-Rubbed BBQ Pork Chops and Bourbon Baked Beans. For a healthful choice, try Beef and Broccoli Stir-Fry paired with Wasabi Mashed Potatoes. Or go all-out exotic with Greek-Style Lamb Burgers and a side of Couscous Tabbouleh. Eating out or eating in, these meats make dinner simply special.

The Meals

Blue Cheese Butter Ribeyes

Start to Finish 20 minutes
Makes 4 servings

Serving Ideas:

Horseradish Mashed Potatoes (below)

Steamed green beans tossed with lemon oil

2 tablespoons extra-virgin olive oil, *Bertolli®*
2 tablespoons Worcestershire sauce, *Lea & Perrins®*
2 tablespoons port wine, *Hardys®*
1 tablespoon Montreal steak seasoning, *McCormick® Grill Mates*
4 8-ounce ribeye steaks

FOR BLUE CHEESE BUTTER:
3 tablespoons butter, softened
3 tablespoons blue cheese, crumbled

1. Preheat broiler. Line a baking sheet or broiler pan with aluminum foil; set aside. For marinade, in a small bowl, combine olive oil, Worcestershire sauce, port wine, and steak seasoning; set aside.

2. Place steaks on a platter and pour marinade over steaks. Prick each steak several times with a fork so that marinade works its way into the meat. Turn steaks over and repeat. Let steaks stand.

3. Meanwhile, for Blue Cheese Butter, in a small bowl, mash together the softened butter and blue cheese with a fork; set aside.

4. Broil steaks 4 to 6 inches from heat for 5 to 7 minutes per side for medium (160 degrees F). Serve steaks with Blue Cheese Butter.

Horseradish Mashed Potatoes

Start to Finish 10 minutes
Makes 4 servings

1 container (24-ounce) homestyle mashed potatoes, *Country Crock®*
2 tablespoons sour cream, *Knudsen®*
1 tablespoon prepared horseradish
1 teaspoon Worcestershire sauce, *Lea & Perrins®*
  Salt
  Ground black pepper

1. Place mashed potatoes in a microwave-safe bowl. Microwave, uncovered, on high setting (100% power) for 3 minutes. Stir in sour cream, horseradish, and Worcestershire sauce.

2. Microwave for 3 minutes more. Season with salt and pepper. Serve hot.

Southwestern Steak Salad with Chipotle Ranch Dressing

Start to Finish 20 minutes
Makes 4 servings

Serving Ideas:
Tortilla Soup (page 73)

Warm flour tortillas
with butter

2	tablespoons extra-virgin olive oil, *Bertolli*
1	pound flank steak, cut across the grain into thin strips
2	tablespoons taco seasoning mix, *McCormick®*

FOR CHIPOTLE RANCH DRESSING:

¼	cup ranch salad dressing, *Hidden Valley®*
¼	cup bottled chipotle salsa, *Pace®*

FOR SOUTHWESTERN STEAK SALAD:

	Tortilla chips, *Mission®*
9	ounces prewashed salad mix, *Ready Pac®*
1	can (11-ounce) mexicorn, drained, *Green Giant®*
1	cup shredded Mexican cheese blend, *Sargento®*
1	avocado, sliced
2	medium tomatoes, diced
¼	cup real bacon pieces, *Hormel®* (optional)
	Nacho sliced jalapeños, *Embasa®* (optional)

1. In a large skillet, heat olive oil over medium-high heat. Sprinkle steak strips with taco seasoning mix. Add steak strips to hot oil; cook and stir for 5 to 7 minutes or until cooked through.

2. For Chipotle Ranch Dressing, in a small bowl, combine salad dressing and salsa. Set aside.

3. For Southwestern Steak Salad, spread a handful of chips on each of 4 salad plates. Add some of the salad mix to each plate. Top with some of the drained mexicorn and cheese. Divide steak strips among plates. Top each plate with some of the avocado and diced tomatoes. Garnish plates with bacon pieces and nacho sliced jalapeños (optional). Serve with Chipotle Ranch Dressing.

Tortilla Soup

Tortilla chips soak up creamy ranchero soup, corn, and Mexican-style tomatoes in a simplified version of everybody's south-of-the-border favorite. Add chunks of leftover chicken to make it a one-dish dinner. Muy bueno!

1	tablespoon extra-virgin olive oil, *Bertolli®*
1	cup diced red onion
2	teaspoons bottled minced garlic, *Christopher Ranch®*
1	container (32-ounce) reduced-sodium chicken broth, *Swanson®*
1	can (10.75-ounce) condensed creamy ranchero soup, *Campbell's®*
1	can (10.75-ounce) Mexican-style tomatoes, *Ro-Tel® Mexican Fiesta*
1	cup loose-pack frozen whole-kernel corn, *C&W®*
½	cup tortilla chips, crumbled, *Mission®*
	Fresh cilantro sprigs (optional)
	Cotija cheese,* crumbled (optional)
	Avocado, diced (optional)
	Whole tortilla chips (optional)

1. In a large pot, heat olive oil over medium-high heat. Add onion to hot oil; cook and stir until soft. Add garlic; cook for 1 minute more.

2. Add chicken broth, soup, tomatoes, frozen corn, and the ½ cup crumbled tortilla chips. Stir to combine. Bring to a boil; reduce heat. Simmer for 10 minutes.

3. Ladle into 4 soup bowls; garnish with cilantro sprigs (optional). Serve with Cotija cheese, avocado, and whole tortilla chips (optional).

*NOTE: Cotija cheese is a firm textured, somewhat crumbly white Mexican cheese. It is traditionally made from goat's milk but also can be made from cow's milk. It is available in Latin grocery stores. If Cotija cheese is not available, substitute Monterey Jack cheese or Monterey Jack cheese with jalapeño chile peppers.

Beef Tips and Artichokes with Merlot and Black Pepper Gravy

Start to Finish 20 minutes
Makes 4 servings

Serving Ideas:
Basil Mashed
Potatoes (below)

Frozen vegetable
medley, heated
and seasoned with
lemon pepper

1   cup Merlot or other red wine
2   packages (17 ounces each) beef tips with gravy, *Tyson®*
1   box (8-ounce) frozen artichoke hearts, *C&W®*
2   teaspoons Montreal steak seasoning, *McCormick® Grill Mates*
2   teaspoons cracked black peppercorns

1. In a medium saucepan, bring Merlot to a boil over medium-high heat. Boil for 4 to 5 minutes or until liquid is reduced by half.

2. Add beef tips with gravy, frozen artichoke hearts, steak seasoning, and peppercorns to saucepan. Bring to simmer; cook for 8 to 10 minutes or until heated through. Serve hot.

Basil Mashed Potatoes

Start to Finish 10 minutes
Makes 4 servings

1   container (24-ounce) homestyle mashed potatoes, *Country Crock®*
1   tablespoon prepared pesto, *Classico®*
$\frac{1}{4}$ cup finely chopped fresh basil

1. Place mashed potatoes in a microwave-safe bowl. Microwave, uncovered, on high setting (100% power) for 3 minutes. Stir; microwave for 2 to 3 minutes more.

2. Stir in pesto and basil. Serve hot.

Beef Burgundy

Start to Finish 20 minutes
Makes 6 servings

Serving Ideas:
Parsleyed Egg
Noodles (below)

Prewashed spring
lettuce mix with bottled
raspberry vinaigrette

4	slices thick-sliced bacon, diced
1	package (17-ounce) beef tips in gravy, *Tyson®*
1	can (14.5-ounce) diced tomatoes with basil, garlic, and oregano, *Del Monte®*
1	package (8-ounce) presliced fresh white button mushrooms
1	cup loose-pack frozen carrot slices, *C&W®*
1	cup loose-pack frozen or bottled pearl onions
1	cup Merlot, Pinot Noir, or other red wine
2	tablespoons tomato paste, *Hunt's®*
	Fresh parsley, chopped (optional)

1. In a large skillet, brown diced bacon over medium heat. Drain and discard bacon fat. Set aside some of the bacon for garnish (optional). To the remaining bacon in skillet, add beef tips in gravy, tomatoes, mushrooms, frozen carrots and onions, Merlot, and tomato paste. Bring to a boil; reduce heat to low. Simmer for 10 minutes or until heated through.

2. Serve beef mixture over Parsleyed Egg Noodles (below). Garnish with reserved bacon and chopped parsley (optional).

Parsleyed Egg Noodles

Start to Finish 15 minutes
Makes 6 servings

12	ounces dried wide egg noodles, *American Beauty®*
½	stick (¼ cup) butter
3	tablespoons finely chopped fresh parsley
	Salt
	Ground black pepper

1. In a large pot of boiling salted water, cook noodles according to package directions.* Drain well; return noodles to hot pot.

2. Add butter and parsley; stir to coat noodles. Season with salt and pepper.

*****NOTE:** Cook noodles only until they are al dente. Do not let them get soft and mushy.

Korean BBQ Beef

Start to Finish 20 minutes
Makes 4 servings

Serving Ideas:

Spinach and Lychee
Salad (page 80)

Teriyaki ready rice

Unlike tomato-based recipes originating in the U.S.A., Asian BBQ calls for soy-based teriyaki sauce with sesame seeds and red pepper flakes. A side of Spinach and Lychee Salad meshes perfectly with this sticky-sweet delicacy.

1	cup teriyaki sauce, *Kikkoman®*
3	scallions (green onions), coarsely chopped
2	tablespoons sesame seeds
2	tablespoons dark sesame oil
1	tablespoon soy sauce, *Kikkoman®*
1	teaspoon red pepper flakes, *McCormick®*
1¾	pounds boneless ribeye steak, cut into ¼-inch strips
	Scallion (green onion) strips (optional)

1. For marinade, in a large zip-top plastic bag, combine teriyaki sauce, the 3 chopped scallions, the sesame seeds, sesame oil, soy sauce, and red pepper flakes. Place steak strips in the bag. Squeeze air from bag and seal. Gently massage bag to coat strips; marinate for 10 minutes.

2. Heat a grill pan over high heat. Remove steak strips from marinade; discard marinade. Add steak strips to the grill pan; cook for 2 to 3 minutes per side or until cooked through.

3. Garnish with scallion strips (optional). Serve hot.

GRILL METHOD: Set up grill for direct cooking over high heat. Just prior to cooking, oil the cold grate and place on grill. Remove steak strips from marinade; discard marinade. Place steak strips on grill; cook for 2 to 3 minutes per side or until cooked through. Continue with step 3.

Spinach and Lychee Salad

Start to Finish 15 minutes
Makes 4 servings

FOR DRESSING:

1	can (20-ounce) lychees in syrup
⅓	cup Asian vinaigrette salad dressing, *Newman's Own*®
1	scallion (green onion), finely chopped
1	teaspoon sesame seeds
½	teaspoon red pepper flakes, *McCormick*®

FOR SALAD:

1	package (9-ounce) prewashed baby spinach, *Fresh Express*®
1	can (8-ounce) sliced water chestnuts, drained, *La Choy*®
2	large purchased hard-cooked eggs, peeled and quartered
¼	cup real bacon pieces, *Hormel*®

1. Drain lychees, reserving 2 tablespoons syrup. Set lychees aside.

2. For dressing, in a small container with a tight-fitting lid, combine the reserved syrup, vinaigrette salad dressing, chopped scallion, sesame seeds, and red pepper flakes. Shake vigorously; set aside.

3. For salad, in a large bowl, combine spinach and water chestnuts. Add dressing and toss. Arrange egg slices and lychees on top. Sprinkle with bacon pieces.

Beef and Broccoli Stir-Fry

Start to Finish 20 minutes
Makes 4 servings

Serving Ideas:
Wasabi Mashed Potatoes
(below)

Cold beer (*Tsingtao®*)

12	ounces packaged broccoli florets (see note, page 95)
1	cup loose-pack frozen sliced carrots, *Pictsweet®*
1	jar (4.5-ounce) sliced mushrooms, drained, *Green Giant®*
1	tablespoon water
¾	cup stir-fry sauce, *Kikkoman®*
2	tablespoons dry sherry, *Christian Brothers®*
1	tablespoon soy sauce, *Kikkoman®*
1	teaspoon bottled minced garlic, *Christopher Ranch®*
¼	teaspoon red pepper flakes, *McCormick®*
2	tablespoons canola oil, *Wesson®*
1½	pounds flank steak, cut diagonally into thin strips
½	teaspoon ground black pepper

1. In a medium microwave-safe bowl, combine broccoli, frozen carrots, mushrooms, and the water. Cover with plastic wrap; microwave on high setting (100% power) for 7 to 8 minutes, stirring once halfway through cooking time. Drain well; set aside.

2. For sauce, in a small bowl, combine stir-fry sauce, sherry, soy sauce, garlic, and red pepper flakes. Set aside.

3. In a wok (or large skillet), heat oil over high heat. Season beef with black pepper. Add beef to hot oil; stir-fry for 2 to 3 minutes or until cooked through. Transfer to a plate; set aside.

4. Add drained vegetables to wok; stir-fry for 2 to 3 minutes. Return beef and accumulated juices to wok. Stir sauce and pour into wok. Stir ingredients together, scraping the browned bits from the bottom of the wok. Stir-fry for 1 to 2 minutes more. Serve hot.

Wasabi Mashed Potatoes

Start to Finish 10 minutes
Makes 4 servings

1	container (24-ounce) homestyle mashed potatoes, *Country Crock®*
1½	teaspoons or more prepared wasabi, *S&B®* (see note, page 65)
1	scallion (green onion) (green part only), chopped (optional)

1. Place mashed potatoes in a microwave-safe bowl. Microwave, uncovered, on high setting (100% power) for 3 minutes. Stir; microwave for 2 minutes more.

2. Stir in prepared wasabi. Garnish with scallion (optional). Serve hot.

Pan-Seared Rosemary Pork Chops

Start to Finish 18 minutes
Makes 4 servings

Serving Ideas:
Sweet Potato and Apple Saute (below)

Long grain and wild ready rice

1½   pounds boneless center-cut pork chops
      Salt
      Ground black pepper
⅓   cup Italian-style bread crumbs, *Progresso*®
1   tablespoon finely chopped fresh rosemary
2   tablespoons extra-virgin olive oil, *Bertolli*®
      Fresh rosemary sprigs (optional)

1. Season pork chops with salt and pepper; set aside.

2. In a small bowl, combine bread crumbs and rosemary. Spread mixture on a plate. Press both sides of chops into bread crumb mixture to coat; set aside.

3. In a large skillet, heat olive oil over medium-high heat. Add chops to hot oil; cook for 4 to 6 minutes per side or until cooked through (160 degrees F).

4. Garnish with rosemary sprigs (optional).

Sweet Potato and Apple Saute

Start to Finish 20 minutes
Makes 4 servings

2   tablespoons unsalted butter
2   medium Golden Delicious apples, diced (do not peel)
1   medium onion, diced
2   cans (15 ounces each) sweet potatoes, drained and diced, *Princella*®
½   cup apple juice, *Tree Top*®
1½   teaspoons pumpkin pie spice, *McCormick*®
1   teaspoon cider vinegar, *Heinz*®
¼   teaspoon kosher salt

1. In a large skillet, melt butter over medium-high heat. Add apples and onion to butter; cook and stir about 5 minutes or until tender.

2. Stir in diced sweet potatoes, apple juice, pumpkin pie spice, vinegar, and salt. Bring mixture to a boil; reduce heat. Simmer for 10 minutes or until most of the liquid has evaporated. Serve hot.

Tender Pork Sandwiches

Start to Finish 20 minutes
Makes 4 servings

Serving Ideas:
Creamy Succotash
(page 88)

Potato chips

½ cup cracker meal, *Nabisco®*
1 tablespoon salt-free all-purpose seasoning, *McCormick®*
1 pound pork tenderloin, trimmed, cut into 1-inch slices
Salt
Ground black pepper
¼ cup canola oil, *Wesson®*
4 hamburger buns, split
Lettuce leaves (optional)
Tomato slices (optional)
Pickle slices (optional)
Assorted condiments (optional)

1. On a plate, combine cracker meal and all-purpose seasoning; set aside. Line a plate with paper towels; set aside.

2. Place tenderloin slices between two pieces of waxed paper or plastic wrap. With a meat mallet, pound tenderloin slices ¼ inch to ⅛ inch thick. Season with salt and pepper. Coat both sides of tenderloin slices with cracker mixture.

3. In a large skillet, heat canola oil over medium-high heat. Add tenderloin slices to hot oil; cook for 2 to 3 minutes per side or until cooked through. Transfer to prepared plate.

4. Serve tenderloin slices on hamburger buns. Top with lettuce, tomato, pickles, and assorted condiments (optional).

Creamy Succotash

Start to Finish 15 minutes
Makes 4 servings

1½ cups loose-pack frozen yellow whole-kernel corn, *C&W*®
1½ cups frozen loose-pack cut okra
1 tablespoon water
1 cup milk
3 tablespoons white sauce mix, *Knorr*®
1 can (15-ounce) butter beans, rinsed and drained
1 jar (4-ounce) chopped pimiento, drained, *Dromedary*®
   Fresh thyme sprigs (optional)

1. In a microwave-safe bowl, combine frozen corn, frozen okra, and the water. Cover with plastic wrap; microwave on high setting (100% power) for 7 to 8 minutes or until tender.

2. Meanwhile, in a medium saucepan, whisk together milk and white sauce mix over medium heat. Bring to a boil, whisking constantly. Reduce heat to low; simmer and stir for 1 minute. Remove from heat.

3. Add cooked corn and okra, butter beans, and pimiento to white sauce. Heat through. Garnish with thyme sprigs (optional). Serve hot.

Chili-Rubbed
BBQ Pork Chops

Start to Finish 20 minutes
Makes 4 servings

Serving Ideas:
Bourbon Baked Beans
(below)

Refrigerated macaroni
and cheese, heated,
Country Crock®

Store-bought
corn bread

4	pork loin chops, ¾ to 1 inch thick
	Garlic salt, *Lawry's*®
	Ground black pepper
2	tablespoons chili seasoning, *McCormick*®
½	cup or more bottled barbecue sauce, *KC Masterpiece*®

1. Preheat broiler. Line a baking sheet or broiler pan with aluminum foil. Place chops on baking sheet. Season with garlic salt and pepper. Rub with chili seasoning.

2. Broil chops 6 inches from heat for 4 minutes per side. Brush chops with barbecue sauce; broil for 1 minute. Turn chops and brush with additional barbecue sauce. Broil for 1 minute more or until cooked through (160 degrees F). Serve hot.

Bourbon Baked Beans

Start to Finish 15 minutes
Makes 4 servings

2	cans (16 ounces each) baked beans, drained, *Bush's*®
½	cup chili sauce, *Heinz*®
¼	cup real bacon pieces, *Hormel*®
¼	cup bourbon, *Jim Beam*®
2	tablespoons packed brown sugar
1	tablespoon molasses, *Grandma's*®

1. In a medium saucepan, combine baked beans, chili sauce, bacon pieces, bourbon, brown sugar, and molasses. Bring to a boil over medium-high heat; reduce heat to medium. Cook for 10 minutes. Serve hot.

Sweet and Sour Pork Patties

Start to Finish 20 minutes
Makes 4 servings

Serving Ideas:
Broccoli and Mushrooms in
Oyster Sauce (page 95)

Long grain ready rice

Trade in your ho-hum burger and fries for this colorful pork patty stir-fry.
A tangy sweet and sour sauce imparts outstanding flavor without adding
excessive fat, while the vivid colors of pineapple and red pepper create a
beautiful plate.

1 ¼	pounds ground pork
2	tablespoons soy sauce, *Kikkoman*®
2	teaspoons Asian seasoning blend, *Emeril's*® *Asian Essence*
1	teaspoon bottled crushed garlic, *Christopher Ranch*®
2	tablespoons vegetable oil, *Wesson*
2	cans (8 ounces each) pineapple chunks, drained, *Dole*®
1	bag (6-ounce) frozen red pepper strips, *C&W*®
1	bottle (11.5-ounce) sweet and sour sauce, *Kikkoman*®
	Sliced scallions (green onions) (optional)

1. In a large bowl, combine ground pork, soy sauce, Asian seasoning,
and garlic. Wet hands to prevent sticking; form pork mixture into
sixteen 2-inch patties.

2. In a large skillet, heat vegetable oil over medium-high heat. Add
patties to hot oil; cook for 3 minutes per side or until cooked through
(160 degrees F).* Transfer to a plate; set aside.

3. Add drained pineapple chunks and frozen pepper strips to skillet.
Cook for 2 to 3 minutes or until peppers are just tender. Add sweet
and sour sauce; bring to a boil.

4. Return patties to skillet, turning to coat with sauce. Cover and
simmer for 5 minutes. Serve hot over rice. Garnish with sliced
scallions (optional).

*NOTE: The internal color of a burger is not a reliable doneness indicator.
A patty cooked to its recommended temperature (see specific recipes) is
safe, regardless of color. To measure the doneness of a burger, insert an
instant-read thermometer through the side of the patty to its center.

Broccoli and Mushrooms in Oyster Sauce

Start to Finish 15 minutes
Makes 4 servings

12	ounces packaged broccoli florets*
2	tablespoons canola oil, *Wesson*®
1	jar (4.5-ounce) sliced mushrooms, drained, *Green Giant*®
3	tablespoons oyster sauce, *Kikkoman*®
$\frac{1}{4}$	teaspoon red pepper flakes, *McCormick*®

1. Place broccoli florets in a microwave-safe bowl. Cover with plastic wrap; microwave on high setting (100% power) for 4 minutes.

2. In a large skillet, heat canola oil over medium-high heat. Add broccoli to hot oil; stir-fry for 3 minutes. Add mushrooms; stir-fry for 2 minutes more. Add oyster sauce and red pepper flakes. Stir to coat. Serve hot.

***NOTE:** If packaged broccoli florets aren't available, pick fresh florets up at your supermarket's salad bar.

Apricot Glazed Babyback Ribs

Start to Finish 20 minutes
Makes 4 servings

Serving Ideas:

Cheesy Cauliflower Gratin (page 99)

Prewashed salad mix and bottled vinaigrette salad dressing

Fruit preserves get a kick from Thai chili sauce in this dressed-up departure from traditional BBQ sauce. Precooked ribs make this recipe a sensational snap—just brush with glaze, broil, and serve with Cheesy Cauliflower Gratin.

1	jar (18-ounce) apricot preserves, *Smucker's*®
¼	cup spicy Thai chili sauce, *Thai Kitchen*®
2	packages (26 ounces each) fully cooked babyback ribs

1. Preheat broiler. Line a baking sheet or broiler pan with aluminum foil; set aside. For glaze, in a medium saucepan, combine preserves and chili sauce over medium heat. Cook for 2 to 4 minutes or until heated through; set aside.

2. Remove ribs from packages. If any excess sauce from the package remains on ribs, wipe off. Place ribs, meat sides up, on prepared baking sheet or broiler pan. Broil 6 to 8 inches from the heat for 6 minutes. Turn ribs; brush glaze over back sides of ribs. Broil for 4 minutes. Turn; brush with glaze. Broil for 2 minutes more.

3. Remove ribs from broiler; generously brush both sides with glaze. Cut into serving-size (about 3 to 4 bones) pieces. Serve with remaining glaze on the side.

Cheesy Cauliflower Gratin

Start to Finish 15 minutes
Makes 4 servings

1	can (10.75-ounce) condensed cheddar cheese soup, *Campbell's®*
1	package (10-ounce) frozen cauliflower florets, thawed, *Pictsweet®*
$\frac{1}{4}$	teaspoon cayenne pepper, *McCormick®*
$\frac{1}{4}$	teaspoon salt
$\frac{1}{2}$	cup shredded Mexican cheese blend, *Sargento®*
2	tablespoons grated Parmesan cheese, *DiGiorno®*
2	tablespoons Italian-style bread crumbs, *Progresso®*
1	teaspoon extra-virgin olive oil, *Bertolli®*

1. Preheat broiler. In a microwave-safe, broiler-safe dish, combine soup, cauliflower, cayenne pepper, and salt. Stir in Mexican cheese blend. Cover with plastic wrap; microwave on high setting (100% power) for 6 minutes.

2. In a small bowl, combine Parmesan cheese, bread crumbs, and olive oil. Spoon bread crumb mixture over cauliflower mixture.

3. Broil 6 inches from heat for 1 to 2 minutes until top is golden brown. Serve hot.

Lamb Chops with Roasted Garlic and Mint Aïoli

Start to Finish 20 minutes
Makes 4 servings

Serving Ideas:
Peas and Prosciutto with Mint (below)

Refrigerated garlic mashed potatoes, heated, *Country Crock®*

½	cup extra-virgin olive oil, *Bertolli®*
2	tablespoons finely chopped fresh mint
1	teaspoon bottled minced garlic, *Christopher Ranch®*
½	teaspoon salt
¼	teaspoon ground black pepper
8	lamb chops, ¾ inch thick

FOR MINT AÏOLI:

½	cup mayonnaise, *Hellmann's®* or *Best Foods®*
3	tablespoons finely chopped fresh mint
1	tablespoon extra-virgin olive oil, *Bertolli®*
1	teaspoon bottled minced roasted garlic, *Christopher Ranch®*

1. Preheat broiler. Line a baking sheet or broiler pan with aluminum foil. For marinade, in a large zip-top plastic bag, combine the ½ cup olive oil, the 2 tablespoons mint, the minced garlic, salt, and pepper. Place lamb chops in bag. Squeeze air from bag and seal. Gently massage bag to coat chops; marinate while preparing Mint Aïoli.

2. For Mint Aïoli, in a small bowl, combine mayonnaise, the 3 tablespoons mint, the 1 tablespoon olive oil, and the roasted garlic.

3. Remove chops from marinade; discard marinade. Place chops on prepared pan. Broil chops 4 to 6 inches from heat for 3 to 5 minutes per side for medium (160 degrees F). Serve chops with Mint Aïoli.

GRILL METHOD: Set up grill for direct cooking over high heat. Just prior to cooking, oil the cold grate and place on grill. Prepare as directed in steps 1 and 2. Place chops on grill and cook for 5 to 7 minutes per side for medium doneness (160 degrees F).

Peas and Prosciutto with Mint

Start to Finish 10 minutes
Makes 4 servings

2	tablespoons butter
3	ounces prosciutto, diced
1	package (16-ounce) loose-pack frozen peas, *C&W®*
	Salt and ground black pepper
2	tablespoons finely chopped fresh mint

1. In a large skillet, melt butter over medium heat. Add prosciutto to butter; cook and stir until prosciutto starts to brown but is not crispy.

2. Add frozen peas to skillet. Toss with prosciutto and butter until peas are coated. Cook for 4 to 5 minutes or until peas are tender, stirring occasionally. Season with salt and pepper to taste. Toss with mint.

Curried Lamb Stew

Start to Finish 20 minutes
Makes 6 servings

Serving Ideas:
Cashew Rice with Golden
Raisins (page 105)

Prewashed mixed greens
with bottled balsamic
vinaigrette

Store-bought pita bread

Ground lamb is sauteed in a gentle curry of onions, peas, and cinnamon-flavored applesauce, rendering a stew nuanced with Indian flavor. Cashew Rice with Golden Raisins echoes the sugary undercurrent.

2	tablespoons butter
1½	pounds ground lamb
4	cups frozen chopped onions, *Ore-Ida*®
1	can (14-ounce) reduced-sodium beef broth, *Swanson*®
1	cup cinnamon-flavored applesauce, *Mott's*®
1	package (3.5-ounce) golden curry sauce mix,* *S&B*®
1½	cups frozen peas, *C&W*®
	Sour cream or plain yogurt (optional)
	Curry powder (optional)

1. In a large saucepan, melt butter over medium-high heat. Add ground lamb to butter; cook and stir until brown. Drain fat; discard. Stir in frozen onions, beef broth, and applesauce. Bring to a boil; reduce heat to simmer.

2. Break curry sauce mix into pieces; stir into lamb mixture. Cook and stir about 5 minutes or until mix is dissolved. Add frozen peas; cook for 3 to 5 minutes or until curry has thickened and peas are tender.

3. Ladle stew into bowls. Top each serving of stew with a spoonful of sour cream and sprinkle with curry powder (optional). Serve hot.

*NOTE: Curry sauce mix contains MSG. If you are allergic to MSG, substitute a mixture of 1 tablespoon cornstarch, 1 tablespoon water, and 1¼ teaspoons curry powder. Add it at same time as the mix.

Cashew Rice with Golden Raisins

Start to Finish 20 minutes
Makes 6 servings

3	cups quick-cooking rice, *Uncle Ben's*®
3	cups reduced-sodium chicken broth, *Swanson*®
1½	tablespoons butter
¼	teaspoon salt
1	pinch ground cinnamon, *McCormick*®
1	cup cashew halves and pieces, *Planters*®
¾	cup golden raisins, *Sun-Maid*®
	Chopped fresh cilantro (optional)

1. In a medium saucepan, combine rice, chicken broth, butter, salt, and cinnamon. Bring to a boil over medium heat. Remove from heat; let stand for 7 to 9 minutes.

2. Fluff rice with a fork and stir in cashews and raisins. Garnish with chopped cilantro (optional). Serve hot.

Greek-Style Lamb Burgers

Start to Finish 20 minutes
Makes 4 servings

Serving Ideas:
Couscous Tabbouleh
(below)

FOR BURGERS:

1 1/2	pounds ground lamb
1/3	cup crumbled feta cheese, *Athenos*®
1/4	cup finely chopped red onion
1/4	cup pitted kalamata olives, chopped, *Peloponnese*®
1	tablespoon Greek seasoning, *Spice Islands*®
1	teaspoon bottled crushed garlic, *Christopher Ranch*®
1/2	teaspoon salt

FOR SAUCE:

1/3	cup plain nonfat yogurt, *Alta Dena*®
1/3	cup sour cream, *Knudsen*®
1/3	cup peeled grated English cucumber
1	tablespoon finely chopped fresh mint
4	pita bread rounds
	Diced red onion (optional)

1. Preheat broiler. Line a baking sheet or broiler pan with aluminum foil; set aside.

2. For burgers, in a medium bowl, combine ground lamb, feta cheese, the 1/4 cup onion, olives, Greek seasoning, garlic, and salt. Wet hands to prevent sticking; form lamb mixture into four 3/4-inch-thick patties; place on prepared pan. Broil 4 inches from heat for 5 to 6 minutes per side or until done (160 degrees F; see note, page 92).

3. Meanwhile, for sauce, in a small bowl, combine yogurt, sour cream, grated cucumber, and the mint; set aside. Serve burgers on pita bread; top with sauce. Garnish with diced red onion (optional).

Couscous Tabbouleh

Start to Finish 20 minutes
Makes 4 servings

2	cups reduced-sodium chicken broth, *Swanson*®
1	box (10-ounce) quick-cooking couscous, *Near East*®
5	tablespoons extra-virgin olive oil, *Bertolli*®
2	tablespoons bottled lemon juice, *ReaLemon*®
3/4	teaspoon dried oregano, *McCormick*®
1/4	teaspoon lemon pepper, *Lawry's*®
3	roma tomatoes, seeded and diced
1	cup finely chopped fresh parsley
1/2	cup finely chopped fresh mint

1. In a medium saucepan, bring chicken broth to a boil over medium-high heat. Remove from heat; stir in couscous and 1 tablespoon of the olive oil. Cover; let stand 5 minutes. Spread cooked couscous on a baking sheet; chill for 10 minutes.

2. In a small bowl, whisk together the remaining 1/4 cup oil, the lemon juice, oregano, and lemon pepper; set aside. In a medium bowl, combine couscous, tomatoes, parsley, and mint. Add dressing; toss to combine.

Poultry

Every cook needs a killer chicken dish—perfect for when unexpected guests come knocking at the door. Each recipe in this chapter is destined for compliments, thanks to quick cooking, entrancing flavors, and a knockout presentation. As a whole, they take you on a culinary journey of tastes and textures. From way down south come Cornmeal-Crusted Chicken with Smoky Tomatoes and Southern-Style Greens with Beans. Chicken with Peanut Curry Sauce dishes up the heat of India's curry with the subtle sweetness of Coconut Rice. You'll find paradise on a plate with Caribbean Turkey and Sweet Potato Chili—especially when served with Cheesy Twists for dipping. Simple yet sophisticated, each recipe has the makings of an instant classic.

The Meals

Cornmeal-Crusted Chicken with Smoky Tomatoes

Start to Finish 20 minutes
Makes 4 servings

Serving Ideas:
Southern-Style Greens with Beans (page 113)

Refrigerated macaroni and cheese, heated, *Country Crock®*

½	cup cornmeal
1	teaspoon salt-free all-purpose seasoning, *McCormick®*
1	teaspoon paprika, *McCormick®*
1½	pounds boneless, skinless chicken breast halves
	Salt
	Ground black pepper
3	tablespoons canola oil, *Wesson®*
½	cup Chardonnay or other white wine
1	can (14.5-ounce) diced tomatoes with basil, garlic, and oregano, *Del Monte®*
¼	teaspoon hickory liquid smoke, *Wright's®*
2	tablespoons real bacon pieces, *Hormel®* (optional)

1. In a large zip-top plastic bag, combine cornmeal, all-purpose seasoning, and paprika; set aside.

2. If desired, between two pieces of plastic wrap, pound chicken with a meat mallet to desired thickness. Season chicken with salt and pepper. Add chicken to the zip-top bag. Seal bag; shake to coat chicken. Remove chicken from bag; shake off excess cornmeal mixture. Set aside.

3. In a large skillet, heat canola oil over medium-high heat. Add chicken to hot oil; cook for 3 to 4 minutes per side or until cooked through. Transfer chicken to a plate; set aside.

4. Drain oil from skillet. Return skillet to heat. Add wine to skillet, scraping up any browned bits from pan. Add tomatoes and liquid smoke. Bring to a boil; reduce heat. Simmer about 5 minutes or until liquid is reduced by half.

5. To serve, spoon tomato mixture over chicken. Garnish with bacon (optional).

Southern-Style Greens with Beans

Start to Finish 20 minutes
Makes 4 servings

1	can (27-ounce) collard greens, drained, *Glory Foods*®
1	can (15-ounce) pinto beans, rinsed and drained, *Progresso*®
1	can (14-ounce) reduced-sodium beef broth, *Swanson*®
$\frac{1}{2}$	cup frozen chopped onions, *Ore-Ida*®
$\frac{1}{4}$	cup real bacon pieces, *Hormel*® (plus more for garnish, optional)
2	teaspoons red wine vinegar
$\frac{1}{2}$	teaspoon red pepper flakes, *McCormick*®

1. In a medium saucepan over medium heat, combine collard greens, beans, beef broth, frozen onions, the $\frac{1}{4}$ cup bacon pieces, the vinegar, and red pepper flakes. Cook and stir about 10 minutes or until heated through, stirring occasionally.

2. Garnish with bacon pieces (optional). Serve hot.

Chicken with Apricots and Almonds

Start to Finish 20 minutes
Makes 4 servings

Serving Ideas:
Lemon-Garlic Broccoli
(below)

Chicken-flavored
ready rice

½	cup all-purpose flour
1	teaspoon salt
½	teaspoon lemon pepper, *Lawry's*®
1½	pounds boneless, skinless chicken breast halves
2	tablespoons or more extra-virgin olive oil, *Bertolli*®
2	scallions (green onions), finely chopped
1	jalapeño chile pepper,* sliced thin
1	teaspoon bottled minced ginger, *Christopher Ranch*®
1	teaspoon bottled minced garlic, *Christopher Ranch*®
1	teaspoon shredded lime zest
1	can (15-ounce) apricot halves, *Del Monte*®
¼	cup sliced almonds, toasted, *Planters*® (see note, page 129)

1. In a large zip-top plastic bag, combine flour, salt, and lemon pepper. Add chicken. Seal bag; shake to coat chicken. Remove chicken from bag; shake off excess flour mixture. Set aside.

2. In a skillet, heat olive oil over medium-high heat. Add chicken to hot oil; cook about 3½ to 4 minutes per side or until cooked through (165 degrees F). Transfer chicken to a plate; set aside. Add scallions and jalapeño to skillet. Cook and stir for 1 minute, adding more oil. Add ginger, garlic, and lime zest; cook and stir for 30 seconds.

3. Drain apricots, reserving liquid. Set apricots aside. Add the reserved liquid to the skillet, scraping up browned bits in pan. Return chicken to skillet with any accumulated juices. Add apricots and toasted almonds. Stir to combine; heat through. Serve hot.

*NOTE: Because chile peppers contain volatile oils that can burn your skin and eyes, wear plastic or rubber gloves when working with them. If your bare hands do touch the peppers, wash your hands well.

Lemon-Garlic Broccoli

Start to Finish 10 minutes
Makes 4 servings

12	ounces packaged broccoli florets (see note, page 95)
1	tablespoon lemon olive oil, *O Olive Oil*®
1	tablespoon water
2	teaspoons shredded lemon zest
1	teaspoon bottled minced garlic, *Christopher Ranch*®
2	tablespoons lemon juice, *ReaLemon*®
	Salt and ground black pepper

1. In a microwave-safe bowl, combine broccoli florets, olive oil, the water, the lemon zest, and garlic. Cover bowl with plastic wrap; microwave on high setting (100% power) for 4 to 5 minutes. Check for doneness; cook 1 more minute if necessary. Sprinkle with lemon juice; toss. Season with salt and pepper.

Guava and Rosemary Glazed Chicken Breast

Start to Finish 20 minutes
Makes 4 servings

Serving Ideas:

Saffron Rice with Currants (below)

Steamed sugar snap peas

- ⅓ cup guava jelly, *Knott's*®
- 2 tablespoon bottled lime juice, *ReaLime*®
- 2 fresh rosemary sprigs
- 1 teaspoon bottled crushed garlic, *Christopher Ranch*®
- 1½ pounds boneless, skinless chicken breast halves
  Salt and ground black pepper
- ⅓ cup all-purpose flour
- 2 tablespoons extra-virgin olive oil, *Bertolli*®

1. Preheat broiler. Line a baking sheet or broiler pan with aluminum foil; set aside.

2. In a small saucepan, combine guava jelly, lime juice, rosemary sprigs, and garlic over medium-low heat. Heat through. In a small bowl, strain guava mixture.

3. Season chicken breasts with salt and pepper. In a large zip-top plastic bag, combine chicken and flour. Seal bag; shake to coat chicken. Remove chicken from bag; shake off excess flour.

4. In large skillet, heat olive oil over medium-high heat. Add chicken to hot oil; cook for 3 to 4 minutes per side or until cooked through (165 degrees F). Transfer to baking sheet.

5. Generously brush some of the guava mixture over chicken breasts. Broil 4 to 6 inches from heat for 1 minute. Turn chicken over; broil 1 minute more. Turn chicken over again; broil an additional 1 minute. Brush with remaining guava mixture. Serve hot.

Saffron Rice with Currants

Start to Finish 10 minutes
Makes 4 servings

- 2 cups quick-cooking rice, *Uncle Ben's*®
- 2 cups reduced-sodium chicken broth, *Swanson*®
- ¼ teaspoon salt
  Pinch saffron threads
- 2 tablespoons dried currants, *Sun-Maid*®

1. In a medium saucepan, combine rice, chicken broth, salt, and saffron. Bring to a boil over medium-high heat. Remove from heat; stir in currants. Cover; let stand for 5 to 7 minutes or until liquid is absorbed.

2. Fluff with fork to distribute saffron and currants. Serve hot.

Kahlúa® Jerk Chicken

Start to Finish 20 minutes
Makes 4 servings

Serving Ideas:
Hawaiian Sweet Potatoes
(page 121)

Butter-flavored ready rice

The unlikely combination of jerk seasoning, coffee-flavored Kahlúa,® and chunky peanut butter creates this tasty melting pot of flavors. Make this easy dish on the stovetop and serve with Hawaiian Sweet Potatoes for a laid-back island meal.

1 ½	pounds boneless, skinless chicken breast halves
	Salt
	Ground black pepper
½	cup all-purpose flour
2	tablespoons extra-virgin olive oil, *Bertolli®*
¾	cup Caribbean jerk marinade, *Lawry's®*
¾	cup coffee-flavored liqueur, *Kahlúa®*
2	tablespoons chunky peanut butter, *Laura Scudder's®*
	Fresh flat-leaf parsley sprigs (optional)

1. Season chicken with salt and pepper. In a large zip-top plastic bag, combine chicken and flour. Seal bag; shake to coat chicken. Remove chicken from bag; shake off excess flour.

2. In large skillet, heat olive oil over medium-high heat. Add chicken to hot oil; cook for 4 minutes. Turn chicken; cook for 4 minutes more. Transfer to a plate.

3. For sauce, in the same skillet, combine jerk marinade, coffee-flavored liqueur, and peanut butter. Bring to a boil; reduce heat to low. Add chicken to skillet, making sure all pieces are coated with sauce. Simmer for 5 to 6 minutes or until cooked through (165 degrees F).

4. Garnish with parsley sprigs (optional).

Hawaiian Sweet Potatoes

Start to Finish 15 minutes
Makes 4 servings

1	can (29-ounce) sweet potatoes, *Princella*®
½	stick (¼ cup) butter
1	can (8-ounce) crushed pineapple, undrained, *Dole*®
¼	cup packed brown sugar
2	medium bananas (barely ripe), peeled and diagonally cut into ½-inch pieces
¼	cup chopped macadamia nuts, *Mauna Loa*®

1. Drain sweet potatoes, reserving ¼ cup liquid. Cut sweet potatoes into chunks.

2. In a large skillet, melt butter over medium heat. Add sweet potatoes; cook and stir 1 minute. Add the reserved ¼ cup liquid, the crushed pineapple, and brown sugar to skillet, stirring to combine.

3. Bring mixture to a boil; reduce heat. Simmer for 4 to 5 minutes until liquid thickens slightly. Add banana slices; heat through. Top with macadamia nuts.

Mediterranean
Chicken Burgers

Start to Finish 20 minutes
Makes 4 servings

Serving Ideas:
Bacon and Scallion
Potato Salad with
Balsamic Dressing
(page 125)

Prewashed salad mix
with fresh tomatoes
and kalamata olives

Fresh basil, sun-dried tomatoes, and buttery pine nuts lend the punch of red pesto to health-conscious chicken burgers. Continue the summery theme by serving with heaps of bacon- and scallion-flavored potato salad (page 125).

$\frac{1}{4}$	cup mayonnaise, *Hellmann's®* or *Best Foods®*
2	tablespoons Italian salad dressing, *Wish-Bone®*
$1\frac{1}{4}$	pounds ground chicken
$\frac{1}{2}$	cup garlic and herb bread crumbs, *Progresso®*
$\frac{1}{4}$	cup finely chopped oil-packed, sun-dried tomatoes, *Alessi®*
1	large egg, lightly beaten
2	tablespoons finely chopped fresh basil
2	tablespoons pine nuts (pignolia)
1	teaspoon Italian seasoning, *McCormick®*
$\frac{3}{4}$	teaspoon salt
$\frac{1}{2}$	teaspoon ground black pepper
2	tablespoons extra-virgin olive oil, *Bertolli®*
4	onion kaiser rolls, split
	Lettuce leaves (optional)
	Tomato slices (optional)
	Red onion slices (optional)
	Broccoli or alfalfa sprouts (optional)

1. In a small bowl, mix mayonnaise with Italian salad dressing. Set aside.

2. In a medium bowl, combine ground chicken, bread crumbs, sun-dried tomatoes, egg, basil, pine nuts, Italian seasoning, salt, and pepper. Wet hands to prevent sticking; form chicken mixture into four $\frac{3}{4}$-inch-thick patties.

3. In a large skillet, heat olive oil over medium heat. Add patties to hot oil; cook for 5 to 6 minutes per side or until cooked through (165 degrees F; see note, page 92).

4. Spread mayonnaise mixture on burgers. Serve patties on split onion rolls. Top with lettuce, tomato, red onion, and broccoli sprouts (optional).

Bacon and Scallion Potato Salad with Balsamic Dressing

Start to Finish 10 minutes
Makes 4 servings

1	package (16-ounce) precooked rosemary and garlic potatoes, *Reser's*®
$\frac{1}{3}$	cup mayonnaise, *Hellmann's*® or *Best Foods*®
$\frac{1}{4}$	cup real bacon pieces, *Hormel*® (plus more for garnish, optional)
2	scallions (green onions), finely chopped (plus more for garnish, optional)
1	teaspoon dried tarragon, crushed, *McCormick*®
1	teaspoon bottled crushed garlic, *Christopher Ranch*®
1	teaspoon Dijon mustard, *Grey Poupon*®
1	teaspoon balsamic vinegar

1. Place potatoes in a microwave-safe bowl. Cover with plastic wrap; microwave on high setting (100% power) for 5 to 7 minutes.

2. In a medium bowl, combine mayonnaise, $\frac{1}{4}$ cup bacon pieces, the 2 finely chopped scallions, the tarragon, garlic, mustard, and vinegar. Add cooked potatoes and toss to combine. Garnish with bacon pieces and chopped scallion (optional). Serve warm or chilled.

Szechuan Chicken with Green Beans and Basil

Start to Finish 20 minutes
Makes 4 servings

Serving Ideas:
Scallion Rice (below)

3	cups loose-pack frozen cut green beans, *C&W*®
1	tablespoon water
¼	cup dry sherry, *Christian Brothers*®
¼	cup reduced-sodium chicken broth, *Swanson*®
2	tablespoons soy sauce, *Kikkoman*®
1	tablespoon bottled minced garlic, *Christopher Ranch*®
1	tablespoon dark sesame oil
2	teaspoons Szechuan seasoning, *Spice Islands*®
1½	pounds boneless, skinless chicken breast halves, cut into 1-inch pieces
¼	cup cornstarch
3	tablespoons canola oil, *Wesson*®
¼	cup coarsely chopped fresh basil

1. In a microwave-safe bowl, combine green beans and the water. Cover with plastic wrap; microwave on high setting (100% power) for 7 to 8 minutes or until crisp tender. Drain well.

2. In a small bowl, stir together sherry, chicken broth, soy sauce, garlic, sesame oil, and Szechuan seasoning; set aside. In a large zip-top plastic bag, combine chicken and cornstarch. Seal bag; shake to coat chicken. Remove chicken from bag; shake off excess cornstarch.

3. In a large skillet, heat canola oil over medium-high heat. Add chicken pieces to hot oil; cook about 7 minutes or until cooked through, turning to brown on all sides. Add green beans to skillet; toss with chicken. Add sherry mixture to skillet. Bring to a boil; reduce heat. Simmer for 5 minutes. Stir in basil.

Scallion Rice

Start to Finish 10 minutes
Makes 4 servings

2	scallions (green onions), chopped (plus 1 tablespoon for garnish, optional)
2	cups quick-cooking rice, *Uncle Ben's*®
1¾	cups reduced-sodium chicken broth, *Swanson*®
2	teaspoons dark sesame oil

1. In a medium saucepan, combine the 2 chopped scallions, the rice, chicken broth, and sesame oil. Bring to a boil. Remove from heat; let stand for 5 to 7 minutes or until liquid is absorbed.

2. Fluff rice with fork. Garnish with the 1 tablespoon reserved scallions (optional).

Chicken with Peanut Curry Sauce

Start to Finish 20 minutes
Makes 4 servings

Serving Ideas:

Coconut Rice (below)

Steamed broccoli topped with sesame oil and toasted sesame seeds (see note, below)

2   tablespoons canola oil, *Wesson*®
1½ pounds boneless, skinless chicken breasts halves, cut into 1-inch pieces
    Salt and ground black pepper
2   cups loose-pack frozen cut green beans, *C&W*®
2   cups loose-pack frozen pepper strips, *C&W*®

FOR PEANUT CURRY SAUCE:

1½ cups light coconut milk, *A Taste of Thai*®
½   cup reduced-sodium chicken broth, *Swanson*®
⅓   cup chunky peanut butter, *Laura Scudder's*®
2   tablespoons packed brown sugar
2   tablespoons lime juice, *ReaLime*®
1   tablespoon red curry paste, *Thai Kitchen*®

1. In a large skillet, heat canola oil over medium-high heat. Sprinkle chicken with salt and pepper. Add chicken to hot oil; cook about 5 minutes or until cooked through, stirring occasionally. Add frozen green beans and pepper strips; cook and stir for 3 minutes more.

2. Meanwhile, for Peanut Curry Sauce, in a medium bowl, whisk together coconut milk, chicken broth, peanut butter, brown sugar, lime juice, and red curry paste. Pour into skillet over chicken and vegetables, stirring to combine. Bring to a boil, stirring occasionally. Reduce heat; simmer for 10 minutes.

Coconut Rice

Start to Finish 20 minutes
Makes 4 servings

2   cups quick-cooking rice, *Uncle Ben's*®
1   cup reduced-sodium chicken broth, *Swanson*®
¾   cup light coconut milk, *A Taste of Thai*®
1   tablespoon bottled lime juice, *ReaLime*®
¼   cup flaked coconut, toasted,* *Baker's*®*

1. In a medium saucepan, combine rice, chicken broth, coconut milk, and lime juice. Bring to a boil over medium-high heat. Remove from heat; cover. Let stand for 7 to 9 minutes. Fluff rice with fork and stir in toasted coconut. Serve hot.

***NOTE:** To toast coconut, seeds, or nuts, place in a dry skillet over medium-low heat and stir occasionally until golden brown.

Thai Minced Chicken with Lettuce Cups

Start to Finish 20 minutes
Makes 4 servings

Serving Ideas:
Shrimp Fried Brown Rice
(page 133)

3	packages (6 ounces each) grilled chicken breast strips, *Foster Farms*®
½	cup chopped fresh cilantro
½	medium red onion, diced
¼	cup chopped fresh mint
¼	cup chili sauce, *Heinz*®
2	teaspoons shredded lime zest
¼	cup lime juice, *ReaLime*®
1	tablespoon soy sauce, *Kikkoman*®
1½	teaspoons Thai seasoning, *Spice Islands*®
1	teaspoon bottled minced garlic, *Christopher Ranch*®
1	head Boston or Bibb lettuce, separated into leaves
	Fresh mint sprigs (optional)

1. In a food processor fitted with a metal blade (or in a blender), combine chicken strips, cilantro, red onion, and chopped mint. Pulse until coarsely minced.

2. Transfer chicken mixture to a medium bowl. Stir in chili sauce, lime zest, lime juice, soy sauce, Thai seasoning, and garlic.

3. Serve with lettuce leaves for cups or wrappers. Garnish with mint sprigs (optional).

Shrimp Fried Brown Rice

Start to Finish 10 minutes
Makes 4 servings

2	tablespoons canola oil, *Wesson*®
3	scallions (green onions), thinly sliced diagonally (plus more for garnish, optional)
1	teaspoon bottled minced garlic, *Christopher Ranch*®
2	packages (8.8 ounces each) whole grain brown ready rice, *Uncle Ben's*®
2	teaspoons dark sesame oil
2	large eggs, lightly beaten
4	ounces cooked peeled and deveined bay or other shrimp (if shrimp are large, cut into bite-size pieces)
1	tablespoon soy sauce, *Kikkoman*®

1. In a large skillet, heat canola oil over medium-high heat. Add the 3 sliced scallions and the garlic to hot oil; stir-fry for 1 minute. Add rice; cook and stir for 3 to 4 minutes more.

2. Make a well in the center of the rice. Add sesame oil to the center of the well; heat. Add eggs; stir-fry until scrambled. Stir to combine eggs with rice. Add shrimp and soy sauce. Heat through.

3. Garnish with chopped scallions (optional). Serve hot.

Chicken Chopped Mediterranean Salad with Feta Vinaigrette

Start to Finish 20 minutes
Makes 4 servings

Serving Ideas:
Kalamata and Herb
Focaccia (page 137)

Sauvignon Blanc

1	bag (10-ounce) hearts of romaine, chopped, *Fresh Express*®
2	precooked chicken breasts, diced
1	English cucumber, seeded and chopped (reserve some slices for garnish, optional)
3	roma tomatoes, cut into large pieces (seed, if desired)
1	cup kalamata olives, chopped, *Peloponnese*®
½	medium red onion, chopped (reserve some slices for garnish, optional)
½	cup red wine vinaigrette salad dressing, *Kraft*®
½	cup crumbled feta cheese, *Athenos*®
1	teaspoon Greek seasoning, *Spice Islands*®

1. In a large bowl, combine lettuce, chicken, cucumber, tomatoes, olives, and chopped onion. Set aside.

2. In a small container with a tight-fitting lid, combine salad dressing, feta cheese, and Greek seasoning. Seal and shake vigorously. Pour over romaine mixture; toss to combine.

3. Divide salad among 4 salad plates. Garnish with sliced cucumbers and onions (optional).

Kalamata and Herb Focaccia

Start to Finish 20 minutes
Makes 4 servings

The salty flavor of brine-cured olives from the grocery's deli makes all the difference to biscuit-dough focaccia brushed with olive oil and garlic. Serve as a zippy side or starter for vigorous Mediterranean dishes like Chicken Chopped Mediterranean Salad with Feta Vinaigrette (page 134).

	Canola oil cooking spray, *Mazola® Pure*
3	tablespoons extra-virgin olive oil, *Bertolli®*
1	tablespoon Italian seasoning, *McCormick®*
2	teaspoons bottled minced garlic, *Christopher Ranch®*
1	can (16.3-ounce) refrigerated biscuit dough, *Pillsbury® Grands!*
$\frac{1}{4}$	cup kalamata olives, pitted and coarsely chopped

1. Preheat oven to 350 degrees F. Lightly spray baking sheet with cooking spray; set aside.

2. In a small bowl, combine olive oil, Italian seasoning, and garlic; set aside.

3. Unroll biscuit dough; separate into pieces. Pat each piece into a $\frac{1}{4}$-inch-thick round. Place on prepared baking sheet. Make "dimples" in dough with fingertips. Evenly divide olives between biscuits; gently press into dough. Brush with oil mixture.

4. Bake in preheated oven for 13 to 15 minutes or until golden brown. Cool slightly on a wire rack. Serve warm.

Lemon
Chicken Soup

Start to Finish 15 minutes
Makes 4 servings

Serving Ideas:
Cucumber and Tomato
Salad with Creamy Greek
Dressing (page 141)

Store-bought pita bread,
warmed

Store-bought hummus

3   cans (10.75 ounces each) condensed chicken and rice soup, *Campbell's®*
3   cups reduced-sodium chicken broth, *Swanson®*
$\frac{1}{3}$ cup lemon juice, *ReaLemon®*
3   large egg yolks
1   precooked chicken breast, shredded
1   tablespoon finely chopped fresh parsley (optional)

1. In a large saucepan, combine soup, chicken broth, and lemon juice. Bring to a boil over medium-high heat; reduce heat to simmer.

2. In a small bowl, lightly whisk egg yolks. Gradually whisk $\frac{1}{4}$ cup of the hot broth mixture into egg yolks to prevent curdling. Slowly pour the egg yolk mixture into remaining hot broth mixture, stirring constantly.

3. Stir in chicken; heat through. Stir in parsley (optional). Ladle hot soup into 4 soup bowls.

Cucumber and Tomato Salad with Creamy Greek Dressing

Start to Finish 10 minutes
Makes 4 servings

4	roma tomatoes, diced
1	English cucumber, seeded and diced
1	cup kalamata olives, pitted, *Peloponnese*®
1/4	medium red onion, slivered
1/3	cup plain nonfat yogurt, *Alta Dena*®
1/3	cup Greek salad dressing, *Girard's*®
4	ounces feta cheese, crumbled, *Athenos*®

1. In a large bowl, combine tomatoes, cucumber, olives, and onion; set aside.

2. In a small bowl, stir together yogurt and Greek salad dressing; toss with tomato mixture. Sprinkle with feta cheese.

Turkey Cutlet with Tart Cherry Sauce

Start to Finish 20 minutes
Makes 4 servings

Serving Ideas:

Garlicky Green Beans (below)

Refrigerated or frozen mashed potatoes, heated

1 ½   pounds turkey breast tenderloin, cut into ½-inch slices
        Salt and ground black pepper
½   cup all-purpose flour
3   tablespoons extra-virgin olive oil, *Bertolli®* (plus more if needed)
1 ½   cups Merlot or other red wine
1   can (15-ounce) tart cherries, drained, *Oregon®*
2   tablespoons frozen orange juice concentrate, *Minute Maid®*
1   tablespoon packed brown sugar
2   tablespoons cold butter, cut into 4 pieces

1. Preheat oven to 200 degrees F. Line a baking sheet with aluminum foil. Season turkey with salt and pepper. In a large zip-top plastic bag, combine turkey and flour. Seal bag; shake to coat turkey. Remove turkey from bag; shake off excess flour.

2. In a large skillet, heat olive oil over medium-high heat. Add turkey to hot oil; cook for 3 to 4 minutes per side or until cooked through (165 degrees F), adding additional oil as necessary. Transfer turkey to prepared baking sheet; place in oven to keep warm.

3. Add Merlot to skillet, scraping up any brown bits in pan. Add drained cherries, frozen orange juice concentrate, and brown sugar. Bring to a boil; cook for 1 minute. Reduce heat; swirl in cold butter, one piece at a time, until incorporated.

4. Remove turkey from oven; divide among 4 plates. Pour hot cherry sauce over turkey. Serve hot.

Garlicky Green Beans

Start to Finish 10 minutes
Makes 4 servings

1   package (16-ounce) loose-pack frozen green beans, *C&W®*
1   tablespoon water
1   tablespoon extra-virgin olive oil, *Bertolli®*
4   strips precooked bacon, chopped, *Farmer John®*
6   cloves peeled garlic, thinly sliced, *Christopher Ranch®*
1   tablespoon butter
        Salt and ground black pepper

1. In a microwave-safe bowl, combine green beans and the water. Cover with plastic wrap; microwave on high setting (100% power) for 6 to 8 minutes or until crisp-tender. Drain well.

2. Meanwhile, in a large skillet, heat olive oil over medium heat. Add bacon, garlic, and butter to hot oil. Cook until garlic is a light golden brown (do not let garlic burn). Add beans to skillet; toss to coat. Season with salt and pepper.

Cajun Turkey Burgers with Spicy Scallion Ranch Dressing

Start to Finish 20 minutes
Makes 4 servings

Serving Ideas:
Creole Curly Fries (page 146)

1¼	pounds ground turkey, *Jennie-O®*
1	cup frozen chopped onions and bell peppers, thawed, *Pictsweet®*
¼	cup real bacon pieces, *Hormel®*
2	teaspoons Cajun seasoning, *McCormick®*
½	teaspoon salt
½	teaspoon ground black pepper
½	teaspoon hot pepper sauce, *Tabasco®*

FOR SPICY SCALLION RANCH DRESSING:

½	cup ranch salad dressing, *Hidden Valley®*
1	scallion (green onion), finely chopped
1	teaspoon hot pepper sauce, *Tabasco®*
4	onion kaiser rolls, split
	Lettuce leaves (optional)
	Tomato slices (optional)
	Onion slices (optional)

1. Place grill pan on high heat for 2 to 3 minutes or until very hot.

2. In a large bowl, combine ground turkey, onions and bell peppers, bacon, Cajun seasoning, salt, black pepper, and the ½ teaspoon hot pepper sauce. Wet hands to prevent sticking; form turkey mixture into four ¾-inch-thick patties.

3. Place patties in hot grill pan; cook over medium-high heat for 5 to 7 minutes per side or until cooked through (165 degrees F; see note, page 92).

4. For Spicy Scallion Ranch Dressing, in a small bowl, combine ranch salad dressing, scallion, and the 1 teaspoon hot pepper sauce.

5. Serve patties with Spicy Scallion Ranch Dressing on split onion rolls. Top with lettuce, tomato, and onion (optional).

Creole Curly Fries

Start to Finish 15 minutes
Makes 4 servings

Add spunk to packaged curly fries by tossing them with Cajun seasoning and healthful olive oil—the perfect no-fuss complement to Cajun Turkey Burgers with Spicy Scallion Ranch Dressing, page 145. The best part? They only take 15 minutes to make and most of that is the baking time.

2	tablespoons extra-virgin olive oil, *Bertolli®*
1	tablespoon Cajun seasoning, *McCormick®*
1	teaspoon salt
½	bag (28-ounce) curly fries, *Ore-Ida®*
	Chili sauce, *Heinz®*

1. Preheat broiler. Line a baking sheet or broiler pan with aluminum foil; set aside.

2. In a small bowl, combine olive oil, Cajun seasoning, and salt. In a large bowl, toss olive oil mixture with fries.

3. Spread fries in a single layer on prepared baking sheet. Broil 6 inches from heat for 9 to 11 minutes, turning once. Serve hot with chili sauce.

Smoked Turkey and Pear Salad with Pomegranate Vinaigrette and Prosciutto Croutons

Start to Finish 20 minutes
Makes 4 servings

Serving Ideas:

Roasted Tomato Basil Soup (page 150)

Store-bought baguette-style French bread, warmed

FOR POMEGRANATE VINAIGRETTE:
- 1/4 **cup extra-virgin olive oil, *Bertolli*®**
- 2 **tablespoons pomegranate juice, *Pom*®**
- 2 **tablespoons red wine vinegar**
- 1 **tablespoon garlic and herb salad dressing mix, *Good Seasons*®**

FOR PROSCIUTTO CROUTONS:
- 3 **ounces prosciutto, thinly sliced**

FOR SMOKED TURKEY AND PEAR SALAD:
- 1 **bag (5-ounce) prewashed baby arugula, *Ready Pac*®**
- 12 **ounces smoked cooked turkey breast, thinly sliced and rolled**
- 1 **can (15-ounce) sliced pears, drained, *Del Monte*®**
- 2 **ounces goat cheese, cut into 1/8-inch slices, *Silver Goat*®**
- 1/3 **cup glazed walnuts and almonds, *Emerald*®**

1. For Pomegranate Vinaigrette, in a small bowl, whisk together 3 tablespoons of the olive oil, the pomegranate juice, vinegar, and salad dressing mix; set aside.

2. For Prosciutto Croutons, separate prosciutto slices and roll up slices, starting from short ends. Cut into 1/2-inch pieces. In a medium skillet, heat the remaining 1 tablespoon olive oil over medium-high heat. Add rolled prosciutto pieces to hot oil; cook for 3 to 4 minutes or until brown on all sides. Using a slotted spoon remove prosciutto from skillet; drain on paper towels.

3. For Smoked Turkey and Pear Salad, divide the arugula among 4 salad plates. Top each portion with rolled turkey slices, pear slices, goat cheese, glazed nuts, and Prosciutto Croutons. Drizzle with Pomegranate Vinaigrette.

Roasted Tomato-Basil Soup

Start to Finish 15 minutes
Makes 4 servings

2	tablespoons extra-virgin olive oil, *Bertolli*®
$\frac{1}{4}$	cup frozen chopped onion, *Ore-Ida*®
1	teaspoon bottled minced garlic, *Christopher Ranch*®
3	cans (14.5 ounces each) fire-roasted diced tomatoes, *Muir Glen*®
$\frac{1}{2}$	cup dry vermouth
$\frac{1}{2}$	cup reduced-sodium chicken broth, *Swanson*®
10	large fresh basil leaves
$\frac{1}{4}$	teaspoon salt
	Salt
	Ground black pepper
$\frac{1}{2}$	cup whipping cream
	Coarsely chopped fresh basil (optional)

1. In a large saucepan, heat olive oil over medium-high heat. Add onion and garlic to hot oil; cook and stir for 1 minute.

2. Add tomatoes, vermouth, chicken broth, the 10 basil leaves, and the $\frac{1}{4}$ teaspoon salt. Bring to a boil; reduce heat. Simmer for 5 minutes; remove from heat.

3. Working in batches, puree mixture in blender.* Season with additional salt and pepper. Return puree to saucepan. Add whipping cream and heat through. Garnish with chopped basil (optional). Serve hot.

*****NOTE:** When blending hot liquids, fill the blender bowl only half full and place a kitchen towel over the lid. Always start with lower blender settings before moving to the puree setting. Or, if desired, use a handheld immersion blender to puree the mixture (see photo, page 13).

Caribbean Turkey and Sweet Potato Chili

Start to Finish 20 minutes
Makes 4 servings

Serving Ideas:
Cheesy Twists (page 154) or store-bought corn bread with honey butter

Mango nectar mingles with sweet potatoes and black beans to give this high-fiber turkey stew a brilliant fusion of flavors, colors, and textures. To round out the meal, serve with a batch of Cheesy Twists or store-bought corn bread with honey butter.

1 tablespoon extra-virgin olive oil, *Bertolli®*
1¼ pounds ground turkey breast, *Jennie-O®*
1 teaspoon bottled minced garlic, *Christopher Ranch®*
1 can (15-ounce) reduced-sodium black beans, rinsed and drained, *S&W®*
1 can (15-ounce) sweet potatoes, diced, *Princella®*
1 can (14.5-ounce) diced tomatoes with green pepper and onion, *Del Monte®*
1 can (14.5-ounce) reduced-sodium chicken broth, *Swanson®*
1 cup mango nectar, *Kerns®*
1 packet (1.25-ounce) mild chili seasoning mix, *McCormick®*
½ teaspoon ground allspice, *McCormick®*
Chopped fresh cilantro (optional)

1. In a large skillet, heat olive oil over medium-high heat. Add ground turkey and garlic to hot oil; cook and stir about 5 minutes or until turkey is cooked through.

2. Add black beans, sweet potatoes, tomatoes, chicken broth, mango nectar, chili seasoning mix, and allspice to cooked turkey; stir to combine. Bring mixture to a boil; reduce heat. Simmer for 10 minutes or until liquid has thickened.

3. Ladle into 4 soup bowls. Garnish with cilantro (optional).

Cheesy Twists

Start to Finish 20 minutes
Makes 4 servings (12 twists)

½ **package frozen puff pastry, thawed, *Pepperidge Farm*®**
1 **large egg**
1 **tablespoon water**
½ **cup grated Parmesan cheese, *DiGiorno*®**

1. Preheat oven to 400 degrees F. Line a baking sheet with aluminum foil; set aside. Unfold thawed puff pastry onto a cutting board.

2. In a small bowl, lightly beat egg and the water with a fork. Using a pastry brush, lightly brush half the egg mixture over puff pastry. Sprinkle with ¼ cup Parmesan cheese; gently pat down so the cheese sticks to pastry. Carefully turn over pastry and repeat with remaining egg mixture and Parmesan cheese.

3. Using a pizza cutter, cut pastry into 1-inch-wide strips. Twist each strip by turning the ends in opposite directions. Arrange evenly on prepared baking sheet.

4. Bake for 15 minutes or until twists are golden brown. Remove from oven; transfer twists to a wire rack. Serve warm.

Fish

The saying "live by the sea; eat from the sea" couldn't be more accurate! When I was growing up in a small town outside of Seattle, I acquired a taste for fresh fish, and now I can't imagine going long without it. I have many reasons to love seafood—it's healthful, a breeze to cook, and when creatively sauced, it makes a splash at any gathering. These recipes include a medley of tastes I adored as a child and those I discovered as an adult. Some, like Oyster Stew, embrace the traditional; others, like Salmon and Goat Cheese Burritos, introduce adventuresome pairings. Sauces work with sides to highlight the natural flavors of the fish: Poached Sole with Champagne Sauce alongside Lemon-Herb Orzo, Shrimp Chiles Rellenos paired with Baja-Style Corn, and Broiled Salmon with Pesto Mayonnaise served with a side of Tuscan White Beans with Tomatoes are perfect examples. Fish is the original fast food—cook a few minutes on each side and dinner is served!

The Meals

Broiled Salmon with Pesto Mayonnaise

Start to Finish 20 minutes
Makes 4 servings

Serving Ideas:

Tuscan White Beans with Tomatoes (below)

Purchased baby spinach mixed with marinated artichoke hearts, tomatoes, and bottled vinaigrette dressing

1 ½ pounds center-cut fresh salmon fillet, 1 inch thick, cut into 4 pieces
¼ cup extra-virgin olive oil, *Bertolli*®
2 tablespoons bottled lemon juice, *ReaLemon*®
2 teaspoons Italian seasoning, *McCormick*®

FOR PESTO MAYONNAISE:
3 tablespoons mayonnaise, *Hellmann's*® or *Best Foods*®
1 tablespoon prepared pesto, *Classico*®

1. Preheat broiler. Rinse salmon with cold water; pat dry with paper towels. Line baking sheet or broiler pan with aluminum foil; set aside.

2. For marinade, in a large zip-top plastic bag, combine olive oil, lemon juice, and Italian seasoning. Add salmon. Squeeze air from bag and seal. Gently massage bag to coat fish; set aside.

3. For Pesto Mayonnaise, in a small bowl, stir together mayonnaise and pesto; set aside. Remove salmon pieces from the bag and place, flesh sides down, on prepared baking sheet. Discard marinade. Broil fish 4 to 6 inches from heat for 3 to 4 minutes. Turn salmon; cook for 4 to 6 minutes more or until fish flakes easily when tested with a fork. Serve salmon with Pesto Mayonnaise.

Tuscan White Beans with Tomatoes

Start to Finish 15 minutes
Makes 4 servings

2 cans (15 ounces each) cannellini beans, rinsed and drained, *Progresso*®
1 can (14.5-ounce) diced tomatoes with basil, garlic, and oregano, drained, *Del Monte*®
1 cup reduced-sodium chicken broth, *Swanson*®
3 tablespoons extra-virgin olive oil, *Bertolli*®
  Salt and ground black pepper
  Grated Romano cheese (optional)

1. In a medium saucepan, combine cannellini beans, tomatoes, chicken broth, and olive oil. Bring to a boil over medium-high heat; reduce heat to medium. Simmer for 8 to 10 minutes or until broth thickens.

2. Season with salt and pepper. Garnish with Romano cheese (optional). Serve hot.

Salmon and Goat Cheese Burritos

Start to Finish 20 minutes
Makes 4 servings

Serving Ideas:
Cucumber-Tomato-Avocado Salad with Tequila-Lime Vinaigrette (below)

1	**1-pound fresh salmon fillet**
2	**teaspoons extra-virgin olive oil, *Bertolli*®**
1	**teaspoon Mexican seasoning, *McCormick*®**
1	**can (15-ounce) reduced-sodium black beans, rinsed and drained, *S&W*®**
1	**cup bottled peach salsa, *Mrs. Renfro's*® (plus more for serving, optional)**
4	**burrito-size flour tortillas, *Mission*®**
8	**ounces soft goat cheese**

1. Preheat broiler. Rinse salmon with cold water; pat dry. Line a broiler pan with aluminum foil. Rub olive oil over both sides of salmon. Sprinkle with Mexican seasoning. Place salmon, skin side up, on prepared broiler pan. Broil 6 inches from heat for 3 minutes. Turn salmon; broil for 5 to 6 minutes more or until fish flakes easily when tested with a fork. Remove from oven. Remove skin; flake into large pieces. Meanwhile, in a medium saucepan, combine beans and peach salsa over medium heat. Bring to a simmer; reduce heat. Keep warm.

2. To make each burrito, microwave one tortilla on high setting (100% power) for 15 seconds. Spread center of tortilla with 2 ounces (about 2 tablespoons) of goat cheese. Add one-fourth of the black beans and salsa. Top with one-fourth of the salmon. Fold tortilla sides over salmon; roll up. Repeat with remaining ingredients. Serve with additional salsa (optional).

Cucumber-Tomato-Avocado Salad with Tequila-Lime Vinaigrette

Start to Finish 15 minutes
Makes 4 servings

FOR CUCUMBER-TOMATO-AVOCADO SALAD:

1	**English cucumber, peeled and chopped**
2	**medium tomatoes, diced**
1	**avocado, diced**

FOR TEQUILA-LIME VINAIGRETTE:

3	**tablespoons extra-virgin olive oil, *Bertolli*®**
1	**tablespoon bottled lime juice, *ReaLime*®**
2	**teaspoons tequila**
¾	**teaspoon garlic and herb salad dressing mix, *Good Seasons*®**

1. For Cucumber-Tomato-Avocado Salad, in a medium bowl, combine cucumber, tomato, and avocado.

2. For Tequila-Lime Vinaigrette, in a small container with a tight-fitting lid, combine olive oil, lime juice, tequila, and salad dressing mix. Shake vigorously. Pour vinaigrette over salad; lightly toss.

Macadamia-Crusted Halibut with Pineapple Salsa

Start to Finish 20 minutes
Makes 4 servings

Serving Ideas:
Roasted Asparagus with Cashew-Curry Mayonnaise (page 165)

Rice pilaf ready rice

A macadamia nut crust ensures the halibut underneath remains flake-away tender. Topped with piquant pineapple salsa and plated alongside crunchy cashew-curry asparagus, it's impressive enough for company. But why wait? Treat yourself tonight!

FOR MACADAMIA-CRUSTED HALIBUT:

4	6-ounce fresh halibut steaks, 1 inch thick
¾	cup chopped macadamia nuts, *Mauna Loa®*
1	large egg, lightly beaten
1	tablespoon water
½	cup all-purpose flour
	Salt
	Ground black pepper

FOR PINEAPPLE SALSA:

2	cans (8 ounces each) crushed pineapple, drained, *Dole®*
¼	cup finely chopped red onion
2	tablespoons roasted red peppers, chopped, *Delallo®*
2	tablespoons finely chopped fresh cilantro
2	tablespoons bottled lime juice, *ReaLime®*
	Pinch salt

1. Preheat oven to 425 degrees F. Rinse halibut with cold water; pat dry with paper towels. Set aside. Line a baking sheet with aluminum foil; set aside.

2. For Macadamia-Crusted Halibut, place macadamia nuts in a shallow bowl. In a second shallow bowl, beat together egg and the water. Place flour in a third shallow bowl. Season halibut with salt and black pepper. Dredge halibut in flour; shake off excess. Dip in egg mixture. Lightly coat with macadamia nuts. Place halibut on prepared baking sheet.

3. Bake halibut in preheated oven for 10 to 12 minutes or until fish flakes easily when tested with a fork.

4. Meanwhile, for Pineapple Salsa, in a small bowl, combine pineapple, onion, red peppers, cilantro, lime juice, and the pinch salt. Set aside.

5. Serve Macadamia-Crusted Halibut with Pineapple Salsa.

Roasted Asparagus with Cashew-Curry Mayonnaise

Start to Finish 20 minutes
Makes 4 servings

1	pound asparagus spears, trimmed
2	teaspoons extra-virgin olive oil, *Bertolli*®
	Salt
	Ground black pepper
2	tablespoons cashews, *Planters*®
½	cup light mayonnaise, *Hellmann's*® or *Best Foods*®
1	teaspoon curry powder, *McCormick*®
½	teaspoon bottled lemon juice, *ReaLemon*®
	Pinch salt
	Cashews (optional)

1. Preheat oven to 425 degrees F. Line a baking sheet with aluminum foil.

2. Place asparagus on prepared baking sheet; drizzle with olive oil. Season with salt and pepper. Toss to evenly distribute oil and seasonings. Roast in preheated oven for 8 to 10 minutes or until asparagus spears are crisp-tender.

3. Meanwhile, in a blender, process cashews until finely ground. In a small bowl, combine ground cashews, mayonnaise, curry powder, lemon juice, and the pinch of salt. Set aside.

4. To serve, divide asparagus among 4 salad plates; top with mayonnaise mixture. Garnish with cashews (optional).

Tip: Try doubling or tripling the recipe to use as an hors d'oeuvre for a cocktail party. You can roast the asparagus ahead of time and refrigerate. Serve at room temperature.

Seared Sesame Tuna with Wasabi Ponzu Sauce

Start to Finish 20 minutes
Makes 4 servings

Serving Ideas:
Spinach Saute
(below)

Long grain ready rice

1 ½   pounds fresh tuna steaks, 1 inch thick
⅓   cup ponzu sauce,* *Maruchan*®
¾   teaspoon prepared wasabi, *S&B*® (see note, page 65)
¼   cup sesame seeds
2   tablespoons canola oil, *Wesson*®

1. Rinse tuna with cold water; pat dry with paper towels. Set aside. In a small bowl, mix together ponzu sauce and wasabi until wasabi is incorporated and there are no lumps; set aside. Spread sesame seeds on a plate or pie pan. Press both sides of the tuna steaks into sesame seeds to coat.

2. In a large skillet, heat canola oil over medium-high heat. Add the tuna to hot oil; cook for 3 to 5 minutes per side, depending on desired doneness of tuna. (Be careful not to overcook the tuna as it will dry out quickly.) Serve wasabi mixture with fish.

*NOTE: Ponzu (PON-zoo) sauce is a Japanese sauce usually made from lemon juice, soy sauce, and other ingredients. You'll find it in the Asian section of the grocery store or in natural food stores or Asian groceries.

Spinach Saute

Start to Finish 10 minutes
Makes 4 servings

2   tablespoons extra-virgin olive oil, *Bertolli*®
1   cup frozen diced onions, *Ore-Ida*®
1   teaspoon bottled crushed garlic, *Christopher Ranch*®
12   ounces prewashed baby spinach, *Ready Pac*®
  Salt
  Ground black pepper

1. In a large skillet, heat olive oil over medium heat. Add the frozen onions and the garlic to hot oil; cook for 2 minutes.

2. Turn heat to medium-high. Add spinach in handfuls, constantly tossing with tongs as it wilts down. When spinach has completely wilted, remove from heat. Season with salt and pepper.*

*NOTE: Always season any type of wilted greens after they are cooked. Seasoning prior to cooking often leads to overseasoning.

Almond-Crusted Trout with Grand Marnier® Cream

Start to Finish 20 minutes
Makes 4 servings

Serving Ideas:
Orange Couscous with Mint (below)

1½ pounds fresh trout fillets
⅓ cup all-purpose flour
2 large eggs, lightly beaten
2 tablespoons water
¾ cup ground almonds,* *Planters®*
½ cup panko (Japanese-style) bread crumbs
1 tablespoon shredded orange zest
3 tablespoons olive oil, *Bertolli®*
Salt and ground black pepper

FOR GRAND MARNIER® CREAM:
¼ cup orange-flavored liqueur, *Grand Marnier®*
1¼ cups orange juice, *Minute Maid®*
1 package (1.8-ounce) white sauce mix, *Knorr®*

1. Rinse trout with cold water; pat dry with paper towels. Set aside. Place flour in a shallow bowl or pie plate; set aside. In a second shallow bowl, beat together eggs and the water. In a third shallow bowl, combine almonds, panko bread crumbs, and orange zest.

2. In a large skillet, heat olive oil over medium-high heat. Meanwhile, dredge trout in flour; shake off excess. Dip in egg mixture. Coat with almond mixture. Fry almond-crusted trout in hot oil for 2 to 3 minutes per side or until fish flakes easily when tested with a fork. Transfer to plate; set aside.

3. For Grand Marnier® Cream, reduce heat to medium; add Grand Marnier® to skillet, scraping up browned bits from pan. Add orange juice; whisk in white sauce mix. Simmer 2 to 3 minutes or until mixture thickens. Season with salt and pepper. Serve trout with cream sauce.

*Note: For uniform pieces, grind the almonds in a blender.

Orange Couscous with Mint

Start to Finish 15 minutes
Makes 4 servings

1¾ cups reduced-sodium chicken broth, *Swanson®*
¼ cup frozen orange juice concentrate, *Minute Maid®*
1 tablespoon orange olive oil, *O Olive Oil®*
1½ teaspoons salt
1 box (10-ounce) couscous, *Near East®*
⅓ cup chopped fresh mint
¼ cup chopped fresh flat-leaf parsley

1. In a medium saucepan, bring chicken broth, frozen orange juice concentrate, olive oil, and salt to a boil over medium-high heat. Stir in couscous. Cover; remove from heat. Let stand 5 minutes. To serve, fluff couscous with a fork and stir in mint and parsley.

Ancho-Citrus Glazed Snapper

Start to Finish 20 minutes
Makes 4 servings

Serving Ideas:
Tropical Fruit Salad
with Key Lime Yogurt
(page 173)

Long grain ready rice
seasoned with finely
shredded lime zest

Ancho chile peppers are the new chipotle, famous for imparting a smoky flavor and adding zest to citrus. To cool the slight kick from the fish, Tropical Fruit Salad with Key Lime Yogurt is a perfect companion dish.

1 ½   pounds fresh red snapper fillets
⅓   cup bottled Key lime juice, *Nellie & Joe's®*
¼   cup lemon olive oil, *O Olive Oil®*
2   tablespoons frozen orange juice concentrate, thawed, *Minute Maid®*
1   tablespoon sugar
1   teaspoon ancho chile powder, *McCormick®*
    Canola oil cooking spray, *Mazola® Pure*
    Lime slices (optional)
    Whole radishes, washed (optional)

1. Preheat broiler. Rinse red snapper with cold water; pat dry with paper towels.

2. For marinade, in a large zip-top bag, combine Key lime juice, olive oil, orange juice concentrate, sugar, and ancho chile powder. Place red snapper in the plastic bag. Squeeze air from bag and seal. Gently massage bag to coat fish; marinate for 10 minutes.

3. Lightly coat a baking sheet or broiler pan with cooking spray. Remove snapper from marinade and place on prepared baking sheet or broiler pan. Discard marinade. Broil snapper 4 to 6 inches from heat for 5 to 6 minutes or until fish flakes easily when tested with a fork. Garnish with lime slices and radishes (optional).

Tropical Fruit Salad
with Key Lime Yogurt

Start to Finish 10 minutes
Makes 4 servings

1	container (16-ounce) fresh pineapple wedges, diced, *Del Monte*®
1	can (15-ounce) lychees, drained
1	container (8-ounce) fresh red grapefruit segments, drained, *Del Monte*®
8	ounces frozen mango chunks, thawed, *Dole*®
¾	cup fat-free vanilla yogurt, *Dannon*®
2	teaspoons bottled Key lime juice, *Nellie & Joe's*®
	Pinch cayenne pepper, *McCormick*®
½	cup fresh raspberries
	Fresh mint sprigs (optional)

1. In a medium bowl, combine pineapple, lychees, grapefruit, and mango; set aside.

2. In a small bowl, combine yogurt, Key lime juice, and cayenne pepper; set aside.

3. Divide mixed fruit among 4 bowls. Top with yogurt mixture and raspberries. Garnish with fresh mint (optional).

Poached Sole with Champagne Sauce

Start to Finish 20 minutes
Makes 4 servings

Serving Ideas:
Lemon-Herb Orzo
(below)

Steamed asparagus

1 ½ pounds fresh sole fillets
2 tablespoons butter
1 large shallot, finely chopped
1 bottle (750-milliliter) brut champagne, *Korbel*®
2 teaspoons lemon juice, *ReaLemon*®
2 sprigs fresh parsley

FOR CHAMPAGNE SAUCE:
½ cup whipping cream
1 tablespoon white sauce mix, *Knorr*®
Red lumpfish roe (optional)
Lemon wedges (optional)

1. Rinse sole in cold water; pat dry with paper towels. Set aside. In a large straight-sided skillet, melt butter over medium-high heat. Add shallot to butter; cook for 1 to 2 minutes or until soft. Add champagne, lemon juice, and parsley to skillet. Bring to a boil; reduce heat to barely a simmer. Slide sole into liquid; poach for 3 to 4 minutes or until fish flakes easily when tested with a fork. Transfer to a plate; set aside. (Do not empty poaching liquid from skillet; keep at a simmer while preparing sauce.)

2. For Champagne Sauce, ladle ½ cup of the poaching liquid into a small saucepan. Add cream and bring to a boil over medium heat. Reduce heat to low; whisk in white sauce mix. Simmer for 1 minute more, stirring constantly.

3. Return sole to poaching liquid in skillet; heat through. To serve, place sole fillets on plates; drizzle with Champagne Sauce. Garnish with red lumpfish roe (optional). Serve with lemon wedges (optional).

Lemon-Herb Orzo

Start to Finish 15 minutes
Makes 4 servings

1 cup dried orzo
3 tablespoons lemon juice, *ReaLemon*®
2 tablespoons finely chopped fresh parsley
2 tablespoons extra-virgin olive oil, *Bertolli*®
1 tablespoon finely chopped fresh cilantro

1. In a large saucepan of boiling salted water, cook orzo according to package directions. Drain well; transfer to medium bowl.

2. Add lemon juice, parsley, olive oil, and cilantro. Toss to combine.

Chile-Garlic Shrimp

Start to Finish 20 minutes
Makes: 4 servings

Serving Ideas:
Lemony Haricots Verts
(below)

Long grain ready rice

1   **pound peeled and deveined fresh large shrimp**
1   **package (1.6-ounce) buffalo wing seasoning, *McCormick®***
     Bag 'n Season
5   **tablespoons unsalted butter**
2   **teaspoons bottled minced garlic, *Christopher Ranch®***
$\frac{1}{4}$ **teaspoon or more red pepper flakes, *McCormick®***
$\frac{1}{4}$ **cup coarsely chopped fresh cilantro**
2   **teaspoons lime juice, *ReaLime®***
     Lime wedges (optional)

1. Rinse shrimp with cold water; pat dry with paper towels. Remove bag from buffalo wing seasoning packet. Add shrimp and seasoning. Shake to coat; set aside.

2. In a large skillet, combine butter, garlic, and red pepper flakes over medium heat. When butter has melted, turn up heat to medium-high, being careful not to burn butter or garlic.

3. Add shrimp to pan when butter begins to pop and sizzle. Cook and stir for 4 to 5 minutes or until shrimp is opaque and cooked through; do not overcook.

4. Remove pan from heat and stir in cilantro and lime juice. Garnish with lime wedges (optional). Serve hot.

Lemony Haricots Verts

Start to Finish 15 minutes
Makes 4 servings

12   **ounces frozen haricots verts* or petite green beans, *C&W®***
1   **tablespoon butter**
2   **teaspoons shredded lemon zest**
1   **teaspoon lemon pepper, *Lawry's®***
     Salt
     Ground black pepper

1. In a microwave-safe bowl, combine frozen beans, butter, lemon zest, and lemon pepper. Cover with plastic wrap; microwave on high setting (100% power) for 4 minutes. Stir; cook for 3 to 4 minutes more. Season with salt and black pepper to taste.

*Note: Haricots verts are small tender green beans from France.

Rock Shrimp with Spicy Creamy Sauce

Start to Finish 20 minutes
Makes 4 servings

Serving Ideas:

Edamame with Shiitake Mushrooms (page 181)

Quick-cooking miso soup

Long grain ready rice

Creamy mayonnaise keeps the Szechuan spices in this pan-seared shrimp entrée at a low burn. A simple side, such as Edamame with Shiitake Mushrooms, works best with this fiery main dish.

1	pound fresh rock shrimp*
	Vegetable oil, *Wesson*®

FOR SPICY CREAMY SAUCE:

1/2	cup mayonnaise, *Hellmann's*® or *Best Foods*®
1/4	cup plus 1 tablespoon whipping cream
2	teaspoons Szechuan seasoning, *Spice Islands*®
2	cups tempura batter mix,** *Hime*®
1 1/2	cups ice water
	Chopped scallion (green onion) (optional)

1. Rinse rock shrimp with cold water; pat dry with paper towels. Set aside. In a large straight-sided skillet, add vegetable oil until it reaches 2 inches up the side. Heat oil to 375 degrees F.

2. Meanwhile, for Spicy Creamy Sauce, in a small bowl, whisk together mayonnaise, cream, and Szechuan seasoning.

3. Once oil is heated, in a large bowl, combine tempura batter mix and the ice water. Working in small batches, dip rock shrimp in batter; shake off excess. Add to hot oil. (Make sure oil temperature does not fall below 350 degrees F.) Fry for 2 to 4 minutes or until golden brown. With a slotted spoon, remove rock shrimp from oil; drain on paper towels. Skim oil between batches.

4. Garnish Spicy Creamy Sauce with chopped scallion (optional). Serve with warm rock shrimp.

***NOTE:** Rock shrimp look like miniature lobster tails. If rock shrimp are not available, use peeled and deveined shrimp.

****NOTE:** Look for tempura batter mix in the Asian foods section of your supermarket.

Edamame with Shiitake Mushrooms

1	bag (16-ounce) frozen shelled edamame (green soybeans), *C&W*®
3	tablespoons water
2	tablespoons canola oil
4	shiitake mushrooms (stems removed), sliced
1	jar (4.5-ounce) sliced mushrooms, *Green Giant*®
1	teaspoon bottled minced garlic, *Christopher Ranch*®
1	tablespoon fried rice seasoning mix, *Kikkoman*®
1	tablespoon soy sauce, *Kikkoman*®

1. In a microwave-safe bowl, combine frozen edamame and 2 tablespoons of the water. Cover with plastic wrap; microwave on high setting (100% power) for 6 to 8 minutes, stirring halfway through cooking time. Let stand, covered, for 1 minute. Drain well.

2. Meanwhile, in large skillet, heat canola oil over medium-high heat. Add shiitake mushrooms to hot oil; cook and stir for 5 minutes. Reduce heat to medium; add jarred mushrooms, garlic, and cooked edamame, stirring to combine.

3. In a small bowl, dissolve fried rice seasoning in the remaining 1 tablespoon water. Pour into skillet with edamame mixture; add soy sauce. Cook and stir for 2 to 3 minutes or until heated through.

Creole Shrimp Stroganoff

Start to Finish 20 minutes
Makes 4 servings

Serving Ideas:
Cajun Buttered Noodles (below)

Prewashed salad greens with bottled ranch salad dressing

1	pound peeled and deveined fresh medium shrimp
2	tablespoons unsalted butter
6	ounces presliced fresh mushrooms
1	can (14.5-ounce) diced tomatoes with green pepper, celery, and onions, *Hunt's*®
1	can (10.75-ounce) condensed cream of mushroom soup, *Campbell's*® *Healthy Request*
1	teaspoon salt-free all-purpose seasoning, *McCormick*®
¾	teaspoon chili powder, *McCormick*®
¼	teaspoon cayenne, *McCormick*®
½	cup light sour cream, *Knudsen*®
1	recipe Cajun Buttered Noodles (below)

1. Rinse shrimp with cold water; pat dry with paper towels. Set aside. In a large skillet, over medium-high heat, melt butter. Add mushrooms to butter; cook and stir for 5 minutes. Add shrimp; cook and stir for another 3 to 4 minutes or until shrimp are opaque and cooked through; do not overcook. Add tomatoes, soup, salt-free seasoning, chili powder, and cayenne, stirring to combine. Bring to a boil; reduce heat. Simmer for 5 minutes. Stir in sour cream; heat through.

2. Serve hot over Cajun Buttered Noodles.

Cajun Buttered Noodles

Start to Finish 15 minutes
Makes 4 servings

8	ounces dried extra-wide egg noodles, *American Beauty*®
3	tablespoons butter
1½	teaspoons Cajun seasoning, *McCormick*®
½	teaspoon paprika, *McCormick*®

1. In a large pot of boiling salted water, cook egg noodles according to package directions (see note, page 77). Drain well; return to hot pot. Add butter, Cajun seasoning, and paprika; toss to combine.

Shrimp Chile Rellenos

Start to Finish 20 minutes
Makes 4 servings

Serving Ideas:

Baja-Style Corn
(page 187)

Packaged Caesar
salad mix (add a
couple dashes of
hot pepper sauce,
Tabasco®, to the
salad dressing)

Vegetable oil, *Wesson*®
1   can (27-ounce) whole green chiles, drained, *Ortega*®
4   ounces cooked peeled and deveined bay or other
     shrimp, chopped
½   cup shredded Mexican cheese blend, *Sargento*®
1   can (10-ounce) condensed creamy chicken verde soup, *Campbell's*®
1½   cups ice water
1½   cups tempura batter mix, *Hime*® (see note, page 178)
1½   teaspoons Mexican seasoning, *McCormick*®
1   cup bottled cilantro salsa, *Pace*®

1. Line a plate with paper towels. In a large straight-sided skillet, add vegetable oil until it reaches 2 inches up the side. Heat the vegetable oil to 375 degrees F. Select the 8 largest chiles that are not split or torn. Pat dry with paper towels; set aside.

2. In a small bowl, mix together shrimp, cheese, and 3 tablespoons of the chicken verde soup; set aside.

3. In a medium bowl, whisk together the ice water, the tempura batter mix, and Mexican seasoning. (Batter will be slightly lumpy.) Set aside.

4. For sauce, in a small saucepan, combine the remaining soup and the salsa. Cook over medium-low heat until heated through. Keep warm.

5. Spoon shrimp mixture into chiles (use your finger to push the mixture into chile). Do not overstuff or chiles will split. Secure tops with toothpicks.

6. Dip stuffed chiles into batter mixture; shake off excess. In batches, slide the stuffed chiles into hot oil. Fry for 2 to 3 minutes per side. Using a slotted spoon, remove from oil; drain on prepared plate. Serve hot with sauce.

Baja-Style Corn

Start to Finish 15 minutes
Makes 4 servings

Frozen corn goes from boring to extraordinary with the additions of canned tomatoes, lime juice, and fresh cilantro. Although it's delicious when paired with Shrimp Chile Rellenos, page 184, use it as a quick side to complement any Tex-Mex main dish.

2	tablespoons butter
2	cups loose-pack frozen whole-kernel corn, *C&W®*
1	can (10-ounce) diced tomatoes, *Ro-Tel® Original*
$\frac{1}{4}$	cup chopped fresh cilantro
1	tablespoon lime juice, *ReaLime®*
	Fresh cilantro leaves (optional)

1. In a large skillet, melt butter over medium-high heat. Add frozen corn to butter; cook for 4 to 5 minutes. Add diced tomatoes and bring to a simmer.

2. Remove from heat and stir in chopped cilantro and lime juice. Garnish with cilantro leaves (optional). Serve hot.

*Note: If you like, substitute one 15.25-ounce can of no-salt-added whole-kernel corn for frozen whole-kernel corn. Drain the canned corn well, then prepare as directed above.

Killer Shrimp Soup

Start to Finish 20 minutes
Makes 4 servings

Serving Ideas:

Add cooked rice or
angel hair pasta to soup

Mixed Greens with
Orange Vinaigrette
and Sesame-Crusted
Tofu (page 190)

1	cup Chardonnay or other white wine
1	bottle (8-ounce) clam juice, *Snow's®*
1	can (49-ounce) reduced-sodium chicken broth, *Swanson®*
1	can (10.75-ounce) condensed cream of shrimp soup, *Campbell's®*
½	stick (¼ cup) butter
1	tablespoon minced garlic, *Christopher Ranch®*
½	teaspoon or more red pepper flakes, *McCormick®*
½	teaspoon salt-free Italian seasoning, *Spice Hunter®*
1	pound cooked peeled and deveined medium shrimp
	Chopped fresh parsley (optional)
	French bread

1. In a 3- to 4-quart pot, combine Chardonnay and clam juice; bring to a boil over medium-high heat. Cook for 5 minutes. Stir in chicken broth, soup, butter, garlic, red pepper flakes, and Italian seasoning. Return to boil; cook for 10 minutes.

2. Reduce heat to medium-low; add shrimp and heat through.

3. Ladle into 4 soup bowls. Garnish with chopped parsley (optional). Serve with French bread.

Mixed Greens with Orange Vinaigrette and Sesame-Crusted Tofu

Start to Finish 20 minutes
Makes 4 servings

This protein-packed salad satisfies your every textural craving, blending crisp sesame seeds with cheesy tofu and a silky citrus vinaigrette. Pair this refreshing salad with feisty Killer Shrimp Soup for a full-flavored meal.

FOR SESAME-CRUSTED TOFU:
- **14** ounces extra-firm tofu, *House*®
- **2** tablespoons extra-virgin olive oil, *Bertolli*®
- **⅓** cup sesame seeds
- **1** cup roasted garlic teriyaki sauce, *Kikkoman*®
- **½** cup orange juice, *Minute Maid*®
- **1** teaspoon bottled minced ginger, *Christopher Ranch*®

FOR ORANGE VINAIGRETTE:
- **¼** cup red wine vinaigrette salad dressing, *Seven Seas*®
- **¼** cup orange juice, *Minute Maid*®

- **8** ounces mixed greens, *Ready Pac*®
- **1** cup cherry tomatoes, halved

1. For Sesame-Crusted Tofu, drain water from tofu and cut into 8 slices. Place sliced tofu on paper towels to drain; set aside. In a large skillet, heat olive oil over medium-high heat.

2. Spread sesame seeds on a small plate. Gently press one side of a tofu slice into sesame seeds. Repeat with remaining tofu slices. Place tofu in hot oil, sesame seed sides down; cook for 6 to 7 minutes or until golden brown.

3. Meanwhile, in a small bowl, whisk together teriyaki sauce, the ½ cup orange juice, and the ginger; set aside.

4. Carefully turn tofu. Reduce heat to medium; pour teriyaki sauce mixture between slices of tofu. Simmer for 3 to 4 minutes. Remove from heat.

5. For Orange Vinaigrette, in a medium bowl, whisk together salad dressing and the ¼ cup orange juice.

6. Divide greens and cherry tomatoes among 4 salad plates. Top each plate with 2 tofu slices. Serve with Orange Vinaigrette on the side.

Oyster Stew

Start to Finish 15 minutes
Makes 4 servings

Serving Ideas:
Spinach and Citrus Salad
(below)

Store-bought crusty
sourdough bread

1	can (10.75-ounce) condensed cream of potato soup, *Campbell's®*
1	can (10.75-ounce) condensed cream of celery soup, *Campbell's®*
1	bottle (8-ounce) clam juice, *Snow's®*
¾	cup dry sherry, *Christian Brothers®*
2	cans (8 ounces each) whole oysters, undrained, *Chicken of the Sea®*
1	cup loose-pack frozen whole-kernel corn, *C&W®*
¼	teaspoon hot pepper sauce, *Tabasco®*
	Oyster crackers (optional)
	Fresh snipped chives (optional)

1. In a large saucepan, combine cream of potato soup, cream of celery soup, clam juice, and sherry. Bring to a boil over medium-high heat; reduce heat to simmer.

2. Add undrained whole oysters, frozen corn, and hot pepper sauce. Cook for 4 to 5 minutes or until heated through. Ladle into 4 soup bowls.* Garnish with oyster crackers and snipped chives (optional).

***NOTE:** For a special presentation, warm bowls in oven prior to serving. Place tablespoon butter in each warm bowl, then ladle in stew and garnish.

Spinach and Citrus Salad

Start to Finish 15 minutes
Makes 4 servings

1	jar (24-ounce) sun fresh citrus salad, *Del Monte®*
2	tablespoons orange olive oil, *O Olive Oil®*
1	tablespoon chopped fresh tarragon
1	tablespoon chopped fresh chives
1	tablespoon champagne vinegar, *O Olive Oil®*
9	ounces prewashed baby spinach, *Ready Pac®*
	Salt
	Ground black pepper
4	ounces goat cheese, crumbled

1. Drain citrus salad, reserving ¼ cup of the juice. Set salad aside. In a medium bowl, whisk together the reserved juice, olive oil, tarragon, chives, and vinegar. Add spinach; toss.

2. Divide dressed spinach among 4 salad plates. Divide citrus salad among plates. Season with salt and pepper. Top with goat cheese.

Crab and Corn Cakes with Tomatillo Salsa

Start to Finish 20 minutes
Makes 4 servings

Serving Ideas:
Southern-Style Slaw (below)

Hot cooked corn on the cob

3   cans (6 ounces each) lump crabmeat, drained, *Crown Prince*®
1/2   cup mayonnaise, *Hellmann's*® or *Best Foods*®
1/2   cup mexicorn, drained, *Green Giant*®
1/4   cup Italian-style bread crumbs, *Progresso*®
1/4   teaspoon lemon pepper, *Lawry's*®
1/4   teaspoon or more hot pepper sauce, *Tabasco*®
1/3   cup cornmeal
2   tablespoons canola oil, *Wesson*®
1   can (7-ounce) salsa verde,* *Herdez*®

1. Preheat oven to 400 degrees F. Line a baking sheet with aluminum foil; set aside.

2. In a medium bowl, combine crabmeat, mayonnaise, mexicorn, bread crumbs, lemon pepper, and hot pepper sauce. Mix until just combined; set aside.

3. Spread cornmeal over a small plate; set aside. Wet hands to prevent sticking; form crab mixture into 12 cakes. Dredge in cornmeal.

4. In a large skillet, heat canola oil over medium-high heat. Place crab cakes in hot oil and cook about 2 minutes per side.

5. Transfer crab cakes to prepared baking sheet; place in preheated oven for 7 to 8 minutes or until heated through. Serve with salsa verde.

*NOTE: Salsa verde is made with tomatillos. Tomatillos are small green tomatolike fruits covered with a paper husk. They are used often in Mexican and Southwestern cooking.

Southern-Style Slaw

Start to Finish 15 minutes
Makes 4 servings

1/2   cup cider vinegar, *Heinz*®
2   tablespoons sugar
2   tablespoons ranch salad dressing mix, *Hidden Valley*®
1   bag (16-ounce) three-color coleslaw, *Fresh Express*®
1/2   cup chopped fresh cilantro
  Fresh cilantro leaves (optional)

1. In a medium bowl, mix together cider vinegar, sugar, and salad dressing mix. Add coleslaw and cilantro. Toss to coat. Chill for 10 minutes. Garnish with cilantro leaves (optional).

Snacks

Somewhere between breakfast on the run, a power nosh in the afternoon, and a bite before bed, snacks became the fourth meal of the day. Snacks are my not-so-guilty secret. I use the phrase "not so guilty" because these mini meals are a step above, filled with nourishing ingredients, not empty calories. Some, like Corn Cakes with Mango-Peach Pork, are hearty enough to stand alone; others, such as Bacon-Wrapped Artichoke Hearts, make a scrumptious and quick starter to a meal. When you can't stop and sit, Goat Cheese and Guava Quesadillas make a terrific take-along treat. For delicious party foods that are a little different, try Blue Cheese Olive Poppers or Prosciutto-Wrapped Sea Scallops on Wilted Arugula. Keep the makings on hand and whenever hunger hits—or guests show up—you're minutes away from a no-regrets nibble.

The Recipes

Creamy Crab Salad

Start to Finish 15 minutes
Makes 4 servings

For the seafood lovers on your cocktail party guest list, whip up a luscious batch of this rich, elegant meal starter. Served in lettuce leaf cups, it's as fun to eat as it is delicious. If you're having a larger get-together, double or triple the recipe—it'll go fast! Another time, serve this salad as a light lunch for two.

1	package (8-ounce) imitation crab, coarsely chopped, *Louis Kemp*®
1	rib celery, finely chopped
1	jar (2-ounce) chopped pimientos, drained, *Dromedary*®
5	tablespoons mayonnaise, *Hellmann's*® or *Best Foods*®
1	scallion (green onion), finely chopped
½	teaspoon Dijon-style mustard
	Dash hot pepper sauce, *Tabasco*®
	Salt
	Ground black pepper
1	head Bibb or butterhead lettuce

1. In a bowl, combine imitation crab, celery, pimientos, mayonnaise, scallion, mustard, and hot pepper sauce. Season with salt and black pepper.

2. Rinse lettuce, discarding any damaged outer leaves. Pull leaves from lettuce head. To eat, fill each leaf with a spoonful of salad.

*NOTE: If desired, serve salad in a lettuce bowl. To make a lettuce bowl, open up the center of the lettuce head, being careful not to tear leaves. Spoon crab salad into the lettuce bowl. To eat, pull off outer lettuce leaves and fill with a spoonful of salad.

Prosciutto-Wrapped Sea Scallops on Wilted Arugula

Start to Finish 20 minutes
Makes 4 servings

$\frac{1}{3}$	cup dry vermouth
$\frac{3}{4}$	cup reduced-sodium chicken broth, *Swanson*®
3	tablespoons white sauce mix, *Knorr*®
3	tablespoons extra-virgin olive oil, *Bertolli*®
1	package (3-ounce) thinly sliced prosciutto
4	large fresh sea scallops
	All-purpose flour
$\frac{1}{4}$	teaspoon bottled minced garlic, *Christopher Ranch*®
1	bag (5-ounce) baby arugula, *Ready Pac*®

1. Preheat oven to 400 degrees F. In a small saucepan, bring vermouth to a boil over medium heat. Boil until liquid is reduced by half. Add chicken broth and whisk in sauce mix. Stirring constantly, bring sauce mixture to a boil. Reduce heat; simmer for 1 minute. Remove from heat; set aside.

2. In an oven-safe medium skillet, heat 2 tablespoons of the olive oil over medium-high heat.

3. Wrap prosciutto pieces around the outsides of scallops (cut prosciutto to fit as necessary). Secure prosciutto pieces with toothpicks. Lightly dust top and bottom of each wrapped scallop with flour. Cook scallops in hot oil for 1 to 2 minutes per side or until golden brown. Transfer skillet of scallops to preheated oven. Bake for 4 to 5 minutes or until cooked to desired doneness.

4. In a large skillet, heat remaining olive oil over high heat. Add garlic to skillet; stir in arugula. Cook and stir just until arugula is wilted.

5. Place a 3-inch ring mold on a small plate (see note, page 36). Add one-fourth of the wilted arugula; remove mold. Place 1 scallop on top of the arugula. Repeat with remaining arugula and scallops. Lightly drizzle white sauce mixture over tops of scallops. Serve immediately.

Shrimp with Avocado "Ceviche"

Start to Finish 15 minutes
Makes 4 servings

8	ounces cooked peeled and deveined bay or other small shrimp
½	cup refrigerated pico de gallo salsa
2	tablespoons lime juice, *ReaLime*®
2	tablespoons finely chopped fresh cilantro
1	avocado, diced
	Salt
	Ground black pepper

1. In a medium bowl, combine shrimp, salsa, lime juice, and cilantro. Let stand for 5 to 10 minutes.

2. Add avocado; toss to combine. Season with salt and pepper.

Blue Cheese Olive Poppers

Start to Finish 20 minutes
Makes 4 servings

1	cup tempura batter mix, *Hime*® (see note, page 178)
¾	cup ice water
¼	teaspoon cayenne, *McCormick*®
3	tablespoons sour cream, *Knudsen*®
2	tablespoons ranch salad dressing, *Hidden Valley*®
½	teaspoon hot pepper sauce, *Tabasco*®
	Vegetable oil, *Wesson*®
16	large blue-cheese-stuffed olives,* *Santa Barbara*®
	Dash of cayenne pepper, *McCormick*® (optional)

1. In a medium bowl, whisk together tempura batter mix, ice water, and cayenne (batter will be lumpy); set aside.

2. For dipping sauce, in a small bowl, combine sour cream, ranch dressing, and hot pepper sauce; set aside.

3. In a medium saucepan, heat vegetable oil to 375 degrees F. Pat olives dry with paper towels. Dip olives into tempura batter; lightly shake off excess. In batches, carefully place olives in oil. (Do not crowd the pan.) Fry for 3 to 5 minutes or until golden. Remove with slotted spoon; drain on paper towels. Repeat with remaining olives.

4. Garnish dipping sauce with a dash of cayenne pepper (optional). Serve olives with sauce on the side.

*****NOTE:** If you like, substitute any other large stuffed olives.

Antipasto

Antipasto means "before the meal," but this platter of cold cuts and relishes is almost a complete meal in itself. Open a bag of mixed greens and arrange cold cuts, cheeses, and Italian veggies and relishes on top for a simple party appetizer or lunch platter. For extra flavor, drizzle lightly with bottled balsamic vinaigrette—then let the snacking begin!

1	bag (5-ounce) mixed torn salad greens, *Fresh Express*®
1	pound assorted deli meats (such as salami, mortadella ham, and cappocola)
1	container (8-ounce) fresh mozzarella cheese
4	ounces sliced provolone cheese
1	jar (16-ounce) mixed olives, *Giuliano Olive Antipasto*®
2	tomatoes, quartered
1	cup pepperoncini
1	can (15-ounce) garbanzo beans, rinsed and drained, *Progresso*®
½	bottle balsamic vinaigrette, *Newman's Own*®
	Packaged breadsticks (optional)

1. Place greens on a large platter. Arrange deli meats, cheeses, olives, tomatoes, pepperoncini, and garbanzo beans on top.

2. Drizzle with balsamic vinaigrette. Serve with breadsticks (optional).

Bacon-Wrapped Artichoke Hearts

Start to Finish 20 minutes
Makes 4 servings

1	jar (12-ounce) marinated artichoke heart quarters, *Luna Rosa*®
9	slices bacon, cut in half, *Oscar Mayer*®

1. Preheat oven to 425 degrees F. Line a baking sheet with aluminum foil. Drain artichoke heart quarters, reserving liquid.

2. Wrap each artichoke heart quarter with a half-slice bacon. Secure with a toothpick.

3. Place on baking sheet. Drizzle with reserved liquid from artichokes. Roast in preheated oven for 12 to 15 minutes or until lightly browned and cooked through.

Corn Cakes with Mango-Peach Pork

Start to Finish 20 minutes
Makes 4 servings

Vibrant flavors and colors jump-start the palate. Dressed with mango-peach salsa, creamed corn, and sauteed pork, griddle cakes become a visual wow. Using precooked ribs gets this meal from package to plate in no time.

- 1½ pounds precooked pork ribs
- 1½ cups mango and peach salsa,* *Santa Barbara®*
- 1 can (15-ounce) cream-style corn, *Del Monte®*
- 1 box (8.5-ounce) corn muffin mix, *Jiffy®*
- ¼ cup milk
- 1 large egg, lightly beaten
- 2 tablespoons butter, melted
- 1 scallion (green onion) (green part only), finely chopped
- 1 teaspoon chili powder, *McCormick®*
  Canola oil cooking spray, *Mazola® Pure*
  Sour cream, *Knudsen®* (optional)
  Fresh cilantro leaves (optional)

1. Preheat oven to 200 degrees F. Separate ribs and cut meat from bones. Roughly chop or shred meat.

2. In a medium saucepan, combine chopped rib meat and salsa. Cook over medium-low heat until heated through, stirring occasionally.

3. In a medium bowl, combine corn, corn muffin mix, milk, egg, melted butter, scallion, and chili powder.

4. Spray a griddle or large skillet with cooking spray. Heat over medium-high heat until a drop of water sizzles. Make corn cakes by dropping 1 tablespoon batter for each onto hot griddle. Cook for 2 to 3 minutes per side or until golden. Keep warm in preheated oven.

5. Serve each corn cake with a spoonful of pork mixture. Garnish with sour cream and cilantro leaves (optional).

*NOTE: If you can't find mango and peach salsa in your local supermarket, substitute peach salsa in an equal amount.

Goat Cheese and Guava Quesadillas

Start to Finish 20 minutes
Makes 4 servings

8	ounces goat cheese, at room temperature
5	tablespoons guava jelly,* *Knott's®*
8	taco-size flour tortillas, *Mission®*
	Canola oil cooking spray, *Mazola® Pure*
	Crumbled cotija cheese,** (optional) (see note, page 73)
1	cup lime and cilantro salsa, *Pace®*

1. In a small bowl, combine goat cheese and guava jelly just until blended.

2. Spread cheese mixture on 4 tortillas; top with remaining tortillas.

3. Coat a large skillet with cooking spray. Heat over medium-high heat until a drop of water sizzles across the surface. Add 1 quesadilla at a time. Cook until lightly browned. Turn; brown on the second side. Repeat with the remaining quesadillas, adding more cooking spray as needed.

4. Cut quesadillas into wedges; sprinkle with Cotija cheese (optional). Serve with salsa for dipping.

*NOTE: If guava jelly is unavailable, substitute strawberry jelly.

**NOTE: If Cotija cheese is not available, substitute feta cheese.

Red Pepper and Tapenade Slices

Start to Finish 20 minutes
Makes 8 servings

1	can (8-ounce) refrigerated crescent rolls, *Pillsbury®*
$\frac{1}{2}$	cup marinara sauce, *Prego®*
$\frac{1}{2}$	cup shredded Monterey Jack cheese, *Kraft®*
3	tablespoons blue cheese, crumbled
$\frac{1}{4}$	cup olive tapenade, *Cantaré®*
$\frac{1}{3}$	cup roasted red bell pepper, cut into strips, *Delallo®*

1. Preheat oven to 425 degrees F. Unroll crescent roll dough; break into 8 triangles. Arrange triangles on baking sheet.

2. Layer each triangle with some of the marinara sauce, Monterey Jack cheese, blue cheese, olive tapenade, and pepper strips.

3. Bake in preheated oven for 12 to 15 minutes or until edges are golden.

Spinach Soufflé-
Phyllo Cups

Start to Finish 20 minutes
Makes 6 servings

Soufflés have a reputation for being difficult, one these airy snacks easily dispel. Phyllo dough provides a quick-bake crust, while ready-made spinach soufflé is enhanced with cayenne pepper and feta cheese for a tasty filling.

5	sheets phyllo dough, *Athens®*
	Olive oil cooking spray, *Mazola® Pure*
1	tablespoon lemon juice, *ReaLemon®*
1	package (12-ounce) spinach soufflé, *Stouffer's®*
$\frac{1}{4}$	teaspoon salt
$\frac{1}{4}$	teaspoon cayenne pepper, *McCormick®*
1	package (2-ounce) feta cheese, crumbled, *Athenos®*
	Cayenne pepper, *McCormick®* (optional)

1. Preheat oven to 350 degrees F. Lay out 1 sheet of phyllo dough. Spray lightly with cooking spray. Top with another sheet of phyllo dough and spray with cooking spray. Repeat three times more. (Keep stack of phyllo dough covered with plastic wrap to prevent it from drying out.)

2. Cut phyllo stack into six 6-inch squares. Fit each square into a cup of a standard muffin pan. Bake in preheated oven for 10 minutes.

3. Remove plastic cover from spinach soufflé. Microwave on high setting (100% power) for 4 minutes. Remove from microwave. Stir in lemon juice, salt, and cayenne pepper. Return to microwave. Cook for 4 minutes more.

4. Divide spinach mixture among baked phyllo cups. Sprinkle feta cheese on top. Garnish each cup with a dash of cayenne pepper (optional). Bake for 6 minutes.

Desserts

Scrumptious. Sinful. Simple. All the adjectives apply to these fabulous treats. To me, dessert is the ultimate comfort food, a feel-good sweet that soothes even as it satisfies. Put the exclamation mark on a delightful dinner with no-bake desserts such as Orange-Spiced Cheesecake or quick-bake crepes topped with Vanilla-Scented Pears. For double the fun—and triple the flavor—try Triple-Chocolate Double-Strawberry Sundae Sandwiches. A dinner party should end with a fitting finale, such as impressive Lemon Pudding Brûlée, flecked with juicy, good-for-you blueberries, or Apricot Shortcakes lavished with heaps of rich mascarpone cream. Whether it's light and luscious or deep, dark, and decadent, dessert keeps life full and sweet. Share your time, your love, and your dessert with others to experience the sweetest treat of all.

The Recipes

217

Sauteed Bananas over Ice Cream with Oatmeal-Rum Cookies

Start to Finish 20 minutes
Makes 4 servings

FOR OATMEAL-RUM COOKIES:

1	package (17.5-ounce) oatmeal cookie mix, *Betty Crocker*®
1/3	cup canola oil, *Wesson*®
1	large egg, lightly beaten
3	tablespoons dark rum, *Myers's*®

FOR SAUTEED BANANAS:

1/2	stick (1/4 cup) butter
4	medium bananas, underripe, peeled and cut diagonally into 1/2-inch slices
1/4	cup dark rum, *Myers's*®
3	tablespoons packed brown sugar
1/4	teaspoon ground cinnamon, *McCormick*®
1	pint vanilla bean ice cream, *Häagen-Dazs*®

1. Preheat oven to 375 degrees F. For Oatmeal-Rum Cookies, in a large bowl, combine oatmeal cookie mix, canola oil, egg, and the 3 tablespoons rum. Stir to form a dough. Drop dough by rounded teaspoons onto ungreased cookie sheet.*

2. Bake in preheated oven for 9 to 11 minutes or until golden brown. Remove from cookie sheet; cool on a wire rack.

3. Meanwhile, for Sauteed Bananas, in a large skillet, melt butter over medium-high heat. Add bananas to butter; cook for 1 minute. Stir in rum, brown sugar, and cinnamon. Simmer for 3 to 4 minutes.

4. Scoop ice cream into 4 dessert dishes. Spoon banana mixture over ice cream. Serve with Oatmeal-Rum Cookies.

*NOTE: If you like, you can bake only as many cookies as you need. The cookie dough can be covered and stored in the refrigerator for 4 to 5 days.

Ice Cream with Caramelized Pineapple and Macadamia-Coconut Cookies

Start to Finish 20 minutes
Makes 4 servings

FOR CARAMELIZED PINEAPPLE:

1	**can (20-ounce) crushed pineapple, *Dole*®**
½	**cup sugar**
¼	**cup rum, *Bacardi*®**
1	**teaspoon ground cinnamon, *McCormick*®**

FOR MACADAMIA-COCONUT COOKIES:

1	**package (17.5-ounce) sugar cookie mix, *Betty Crocker*®**
¾	**cup flaked coconut, *Baker's*®**
½	**cup chopped macadamia nuts, *Mauna Loa*®**
1	**stick (½ cup) butter, melted**
1	**large egg, lightly beaten**
1	**pint vanilla bean ice cream, *Häagen-Dazs*®**

1. Preheat oven to 375 degrees F. For Caramelized Pineapple, in a large skillet, combine pineapple, sugar, rum, and cinnamon. Bring to a boil over medium-high heat; reduce heat. Simmer for 15 minutes.

2. For Macadamia-Coconut Cookies, in a large bowl, combine sugar cookie mix, coconut, macadamia nuts, butter, and egg. Stir to form a soft dough. Drop dough by rounded teaspoons onto ungreased cookie sheet (see note, page 219).

3. Bake in preheated oven for 8 to 10 minutes or until edges are light golden brown. Remove from oven; cool 1 minute. Remove from cookie sheet; cool on a wire rack.

4. Scoop ice cream into 4 dessert dishes. Spoon pineapple mixture over ice cream. Serve with Macadamia-Coconut Cookies.

Mango Pudding with Triple Ginger Cookies

Start to Finish 20 minutes
Makes 4 servings

FOR TRIPLE GINGER COOKIES:
1   **package (17.5-ounce) sugar cookie mix, *Betty Crocker*®**
1   **stick (½ cup) butter, melted**
1   **large egg, lightly beaten**
2   **tablespoons crystallized ginger, finely chopped, *McCormick*®**
1   **teaspoon bottled minced ginger, *Christopher Ranch*®**
¾   **teaspoon ground ginger, *McCormick*®**

FOR MANGO PUDDING:
1   **can (15-ounce) sliced mango, *Polar*®**
½   **cup or more cold milk**
1   **box (3.4-ounce) instant vanilla pudding mix, *Jell-O*®**
     Frozen whipped topping, thawed, *Cool Whip*®

1. Preheat oven to 375 degrees F. For Triple Ginger Cookies, in a large bowl, combine cookie mix, butter, egg, crystallized ginger, minced ginger, and ground ginger. Stir to form a dough. Drop dough by rounded teaspoons onto ungreased cookie sheet. (See note, page 219.)

2. Bake in preheated oven for 8 to 10 minutes or until edges are golden. Remove from cookie sheet; cool on a wire rack.

3. For Mango Pudding, drain mango slices, reserving liquid. Set reserved liquid aside. Finely dice enough mango to equal ¼ cup; set aside.

4. In a blender, combine the remaining mango and the reserved mango liquid. Cover; puree. Pour mixture into a 2-cup liquid measuring cup. Add enough milk to make 1¾ cups.

5. Place pudding mix in a medium bowl. Add mango-milk mixture; whisk for 2 minutes. Divide into 4 dessert dishes; let stand for 5 minutes. Serve with whipped topping, reserved diced mango, and Triple Ginger Cookies.

Vanilla-Scented Pears

Start to Finish 20 minutes
Makes 4 servings

Top these elegant pudding-filled crepes with ripe pears poached in a vanilla bean-flavored syrup. The aroma and taste are impossible to resist! For a special presentation, serve this dessert in a compote dish and garnish with plump red raspberries and a sprinkle of fresh mint leaves.

1	can (15.25-ounce) sliced pears in honey syrup, *Del Monte®*
2	tablespoons pear-flavored brandy
1	vanilla bean, scraped
1	pack (four 3.5-ounce servings) vanilla pudding, *Hunt's® Snack Pack*
1	package (4.5-ounce) prepared crepes
	Fresh raspberries (optional)
	Fresh mint sprigs (optional)

1. Drain pears, reserving syrup. Set pears aside. In a medium saucepan, combine pear syrup, brandy, and vanilla bean. Bring to a boil over high heat; reduce heat slightly. Boil about 10 minutes or until syrup thickens.

2. Add pear slices. Reduce heat; simmer until pears are heated through. Remove vanilla bean.

3. Spread 1 serving of pudding on each of 4 crepes. Top each serving of pudding with another crepe. Place 1 crepe stack on each of 4 dessert plates. Fold crepe stacks into quarters.

4. Top with pears and syrup. Garnish with raspberries and mint sprigs (optional). Serve warm.

Individual Lime
Cheesecakes

Start to Finish 20 minutes
Makes 6 servings

This recipe is simplicity at its best—and stunning enough for even the most elegant dinner party. Combine bottled lime curd, sugar, and softened cream cheese; scoop it into purchased tart shells; and you're done! If desired, up the elegance of these pretty little tarts by nestling sugared lime garnishes and thin strips of lime zest in clouds of whipped cream.

1   package (8-ounce) cream cheese, softened, *Philadelphia*®
½   cup sugar
3   tablespoons bottled lime curd, *Dickinson's*®
6   graham cracker tart shells, *Keebler*®
     Lime slices, quartered (optional)
     Sugar (optional)
     Frozen whipped topping, thawed, *Cool Whip*®
     Strips of lime zest (optional)

1. In a medium bowl, beat cream cheese and the ½ cup sugar with an electric mixer until creamy. Add lime curd; beat on low speed until just combined.

2. Spoon mixture into tart shells. Place tart shells on a small baking sheet; place in freezer for 10 minutes.

3. Meanwhile, coat lime slice quarters with the remaining sugar (optional); shake off excess. Top each cheesecake with whipped topping. Garnish with sugared lime quarters and strips of lime zest (optional).

Orange-Spiced Cheesecake

Start to Finish 20 minutes
Makes 6 servings

1	box (30-ounce) frozen New York-style cheesecake, *Sara Lee*®
⅓	cup orange marmalade, *Smucker's*®
2	tablespoons orange-flavored liqueur, *Cointreau*®
1	tablespoon frozen orange juice concentrate, *Minute Maid*®
¼	teaspoon five-spice powder, *McCormick*®
1	orange,* sliced

1. Let cheesecake stand at room temperature for at least 15 minutes.**

2. In a large saucepan, combine marmalade, orange-flavored liqueur, frozen orange juice concentrate, and five-spice powder over medium-high heat. Simmer until orange juice concentrate is melted. Add orange slices. Simmer about 10 minutes or until thick and syrupy.

3. Arrange orange slices over top of cake. Spoon warm orange mixture over orange slices. To serve, cut into slices.

***NOTE:** During the holidays, use a blood orange for a festive red touch.

****TIP:** For easier serving, cut cheesecake into slices before adding the orange topping.

Lemon Pudding Brûlée with Blueberries

Start to Finish 20 minutes
Makes 4 servings

A luscious cross between pudding and crème brûlée, this chic dessert blends the tartness of lemon with the sweetness of blueberries. Get all the flavor and prestige of crème brûlée with the simplicity and convenience of instant pudding.

1	box (3.4-ounce) instant lemon pudding mix, *Jell-O*®
2	cups cold milk
½	pint fresh blueberries
¼	cup sugar
	Fresh mint sprigs (optional)

1. Preheat broiler. Place pudding mix in a medium bowl. Add milk; whisk for 2 minutes. Place in the refrigerator for 5 minutes.

2. Count out 12 blueberries; set aside for garnish. Fold remaining berries into the pudding. Divide pudding into four 8-ounce broiler-safe ramekins or soufflé dishes. Refrigerate until ready to serve.

3. Sprinkle 1 tablespoon of the sugar on top of each pudding. Place ramekins on a baking sheet. Broil 6 inches from heat for 2 to 3 minutes or until sugar has caramelized, rotating the baking sheet so the sugar caramelizes evenly.

4. Garnish with mint sprigs (optional). Serve with reserved berries.

Shortcakes with Mascarpone and Brandied Apricots

Start to Finish 20 minutes
Makes 6 servings

1   package (8-ounce) mascarpone cheese, *BelGioioso®*

1   container (8-ounce) frozen extra-creamy whipped topping, thawed, *Cool Whip®*

1   teaspoon shredded lemon zest

½   teaspoon almond extract, *McCormick®*
    Pinch salt

1   package (5-ounce) individual dessert sponge cakes,* *Van De Kamp's®*

1   can (15-ounce) apricot halves in heavy syrup, *Del Monte®*

2   tablespoons brandy, *Christian Brothers®*
    Slivered almonds, toasted (see note, page 129) (optional)

1. In a large bowl, whisk mascarpone cheese to soften. Stir in half of the container of whipped topping, the lemon zest, almond extract, and the pinch of salt. Spoon or pipe (using a pastry bag fitted with a large star tip) cheese mixture into each sponge cake.

2. Drain apricots, reserving syrup. Set apricots aside. In a small saucepan, combine the reserved apricot syrup and brandy over high heat; cook until thick. Add apricots.

3. Spoon apricot mixture over sponge cakes. Spoon or pipe remaining whipped topping over tops of cakes. Garnish with almonds (optional).

*NOTE: If sponge cakes are not available, use sliced pound cake.

Triple-Chocolate Double-Strawberry Sundae Sandwich

Start to Finish 20 minutes
Makes 4 servings

1   package (17.5-ounce) double chocolate chunk cookie mix, *Betty Crocker*®
1   large egg, lightly beaten
¼   cup vegetable oil, *Wesson*®
2   tablespoons chocolate-flavored syrup, *Hershey's*®
1½ cups fresh strawberries, sliced
2   tablespoons or more powdered sugar, *C&H*®
1   pint strawberry ice cream, *Häagen-Dazs*®

1. Preheat oven to 350 degrees F. Grease a cookie sheet; set aside.

2. In a large bowl, combine cookie mix, egg, vegetable oil, and chocolate-flavored syrup. Stir to form a dough. Drop dough by rounded tablespoons onto prepared cookie sheet (see note, page 219).

3. Bake in preheated oven for 12 to 15 minutes or until edges are firm and tops are set. Cool cookies on baking sheet for 1 minute. Remove from cookie sheet; cool on a wire rack.

4. Meanwhile, in a medium bowl, combine sliced strawberries and powdered sugar, mashing lightly.

5. If desired, cut ice cream into squares. Place a cookie on each of 4 dessert plates. Top each cookie with a square (or scoop) of ice cream. Spoon some of the sliced strawberries over ice cream. Top each with a second cookie.

Index

Index

Free
Lifestyle web magazine subscription

Just visit
www.semi-homemade.com
today to subscribe!

Sign yourself and your friends and family up to the semi-homemaker's club today!

Each online issue is filled with fast, easy how-to projects, simple lifestyle solutions, and an abundance of helpful hints and terrific tips. It's the complete go-to magazine for busy people on-the-move.

tables & settings	fashion & beauty	ideas	home & garden	fabulous florals
super suppers	perfect parties		great gatherings	decadent desserts
gifts & giving	details	wines & music	fun favors	semi-homemaker's club

Semi-Homemade.com

making life easier, better, and more enjoyable

Press Kit | Contact Us | Products | Join the Club

Semihomemade.com has hundreds of ways to simplify your life—the easy Semi-Homemade way! You'll find fast ways to de-clutter, try your hand at clever crafts, create terrific tablescapes or decorate indoors and out to make your home and garden superb with style.

We're especially proud of our Semi-Homemakers club: a part of semi-homemade.com which hosts other semihomemakers just like you. The club community shares ideas to make life easier, better, and more manageable with smart tips and hints allowing you time to do what you want! Sign-up and join today—it's free—and sign up your friends and family, too! It's easy the Semi-Homemade way! Visit the site today and start enjoying your busy life!

Sign yourself and your friends and family up to the semi-homemaker's club today!

tablescapes   home   garden   organizing   crafts

everyday & special days   cooking   entertaining   cocktail time

Halloween   Thanksgiving   Christmas   Valentine's   Easter   New Year's

About Sandra Lee

Sandra Lee is a *New York Times* best-selling author and a nationally acclaimed lifestyle expert. Her signature Semi-Homemade approach to cooking, home decorating, gardening, crafting, entertaining, beauty, and fashion offers savvy shortcuts and down-to-earth secrets for creating a beautiful, affordable, and most importantly doable lifestyle.

Sandra Lee's cookbook series offers amazing meals in minutes, fabulous food fixin's, and sensational—yet simple—style ideas. *Semi-Homemade Cooking with Sandra Lee* is one of Food Network's hottest cooking shows, providing many helpful hints, timesaving techniques, tips, and tricks.

Find even more sensible, savvy solutions online at **semihomemade.com**.

Sandra Lee Semi-Homemade® Cookbook Series
Collect all these amazingly helpful, timesaving, and beautiful books!
Look for the series wherever quality books are sold.